Teens' Guide To Financial Independence

Financial Life Lessons For Teens; Advice On How To Get Your First Job And Manage Your Finances Like A Pro

Kev Chilton

PickWood Publishing

Teens' Guide Series

Also by Kev Chilton

Book One – Teens' Guide to Making Friends

Book Two – Teens Guide to Dating

Book Three – Teens' Guide to Health & Mental Wellness

Book Four – Teens' Guide to Financial Independence

Book Five – Teens' Guide to Adult Skills

TEENS' GUIDE TO FINANCIAL INDEPENDENCE

Teens' Guide Book Series

https://kevchilton.com/books

https://kevchilton.com/books

© **Copyright 2024 - All rights reserved.**

The content contained within this book may not be reproduced, duplicated or transmitted without direct written permission from the author or the publisher.

Under no circumstances will any blame or legal responsibility be held against the publisher, or author, for any damages, reparation, or monetary loss due to the information contained within this book, either directly or indirectly.

Legal Notice:

This book is copyright protected. It is only for personal use. You cannot amend, distribute, sell, use, quote or paraphrase any part, or the content within this book, without the consent of the author or publisher.

Disclaimer Notice:

Please note the information contained within this document is for educational and entertainment purposes only. All effort has been executed to present accurate, up to date, reliable, complete information. No warranties of any kind are declared or implied. Readers acknowledge that the author is not engaged in the rendering of legal, financial, medical or professional advice. The content within this book has been derived from various sources. Please consult a licensed professional before attempting any techniques outlined in this book.

By reading this document, the reader agrees that under no circumstances is the author responsible for any losses, direct or indirect, that are incurred as a result of the use of the information contained within this document, including, but not limited to, errors, omissions, or inaccuracies.

Dedication

With thanks to Beth, whose initial conversations gave me the idea to create this five-book series.

A special thanks to Grace for her meticulous research and invaluable advice, which played a pivotal role in creating each book.

To my good friend, Anna, who kept me sane throughout!

Contents

Introduction	1
Getting Your First Job	3
Show me the Money!	
Be Prepared	
Chapter	7
Welcome to the World of Work	
1. What Jobs Can I Do	8
2. How to Sell Yourself	23
3. Interview Techniques	45
4. What Do I Do Now That I'm Here?	57
5. Getting That Work/Life Balance	71
6. Ready to Go Full-Time?	80
Chapter	90
It's All About the Money	
7. Investing, Saving, and All the Hidden Fees	91
8. Budgeting 101	109

9. Grown-Up Expenses	122
10. Financing for University	135
11. Don't Get Sucked In	144
A Final Word	152
References	154
About the Author	161
Teens' Guide Series	164

Introduction

Unless your family is super rich, you must know that you're going to need a job at some point. Without one you won't be able to afford housing, groceries, or to do anything fun with your life. Whether or not you have a clear idea of what career you want doesn't matter right now because you have plenty of time to figure that out. Even if you do know, it's unlikely that that will be the first job you ever get.

Studies have shown that starting to work at an earlier age can improve your career prospects later in life. Someone applying for their first job at 18 or 21 is less likely to be able to demonstrate valuable workplace skills than someone who has been working since they were 16. That could mean they are two to five years behind in reaching career or lifestyle milestones, like becoming a team leader or earning enough to buy a house. (Hunt, 2020).

KEV CHILTON

ESPECIALLY FOR YOU!

FREE BOOKS

Specially prepared books for teens and adults...

https://kevchilton.com/free-books

https://kevchilton.com/free-books

Getting Your First Job

Lots of teenagers start working part-time while they're still studying. School is great for teaching you trigonometry or how many electrons are in a carbon atom, but it doesn't give you real, first-hand experience of the world of work. It doesn't teach you how to deal with a dissatisfied customer, how to use your initiative when unloading a delivery, or how to discuss a raise with your manager. These are all useful skills that will set you apart from other applicants when you're looking for your first full-time job, even if it's in a different industry.

I joined the police cadets at 16, so I didn't get a soft entry into the workplace. By the time I graduated into the police force, I actually had far less experience dealing with people and volatile situations than my friends who had worked in cafes, restaurants, and clothing stores. If I had spent a few months working the till, I would have learned a lot more about calming irate customers, recognizing when someone's lying, and holding my nerve than I did in the classroom or touring with the police cadet football team. By the time I needed to put together a resume and practice my interview technique when applying for promotions and departmental transfers, I was already feeling out of my depth and inferior to the other officers I was competing with.

You might be wondering how you go about getting a job when you don't have any previous experience. What should your resume look like? What happens in a job interview? With so many new things to learn and so many questions, taking that step into employment can seem rather daunting.

What you might not realize is that you already have lots of the skills that employers look for; you just need a little help highlighting them in a killer resume—skills like being responsible, on time, and solving problems. These are things you've learned from school and life experiences, and I'm going to show you how to identify all of your strengths and showcase them in a way that will make you irresistible. We'll also look at some of the different jobs you can do and ways in which you can be your own boss by selling services like dog walking or tutoring.

Show me the Money!

Of course, a part-time job comes with other perks, like wages. Having your own money to manage is a big responsibility and it also starts to teach you financial awareness—something that is a vital part of adulting. What better way to learn about savings, budgeting, and what happens when you overspend than at a time when it doesn't really matter? If you budget wrongly as a 16-year-old, it probably means you won't be able to afford groceries or rent, so make those mistakes now and you'll be a money expert by the time it counts.

Some of you will be looking for a job because you have something specific that you want to save up for. It could be a short-term goal, like gig tickets or a birthday present, or something more long-term like putting money toward university or taking a year out to travel. The sooner you start saving, the easier it is to achieve your goal. Think how hard it might be to save $1,000 for your first car over just six months (an eye-watering $167 a month) versus a year ($83 a month) or even more. It's always a good idea to save money before you need it, then you won't have to wait so long when you do need to buy something.

Be Prepared

The sooner you start working, the sooner you can start saving for the future. You'll also be building valuable skills and investing in your employability. You never know;

the perfect job might be just around the corner, and you want to be prepared so you stand the best chance of getting it. Get your resume written now, even if you don't have a job to apply for. Build soft skills now by working part-time so that you will stand out from other candidates when you apply for the job you really want. Start saving now so you always have a fund to cover unexpected expenses and emergencies and you don't have to scrape together money in a hurry.

What are you waiting for?

Welcome to the World of Work

Chapter One

What Jobs Can I Do

Your work is going to fill a large part of your life, and the only way to be truly satisfied is to do what you believe is great work. And the only way to do great work is to love what you do. –Steve Jobs

One of the best things about your teenage years is that you start to gain some of the perks of being an adult without having to deal with any of the downsides. You're given more freedom to choose and organize your own activities, you can earn money without having to worry about paying taxes, and you can spend it on fun stuff because (most of) you don't need to pay rent or utilities. For most teens, a part-time job funds their social life, grows their wardrobe, or puts fuel in their car, so it's directly linked to getting more enjoyment out of life. You also have more choice about the hours you work and the opportunity to turn something you enjoy into a way to make money.

Once you're an adult, a job becomes something you need rather than something you'd like. I really enjoyed my job, and although I worked for the police for the whole of my career, at different times I had different responsibilities: analyzing data, researching, interviewing suspects, and teaching others, and the job I started with was very different from the job I retired from. What led me to join the police? Ultimately, I needed an income, and if I was going to have to spend 40 hours a week working, I wanted to be doing something that was interesting and helped people. If I'd won the lottery at 18 and didn't need to work, would I still have done it? I think I'd probably have spent more time with my family and enjoying my hobbies instead.

So, if you don't need to work to pay your bills yet, why are you thinking about getting a job? It's an important question to know the answer to because it will help you think about the sort of job you should be looking for. For example, if you want one because you would like to save up for a holiday with friends, you probably need something with regular hours and a reliable monthly wage so that you can budget.

Let's have a look at the top reasons why teens start to look for a part-time job.

Earn Money

Having your own income that you control is a big milestone on the way to growing up. Even if it's only a small amount and for small things, being able to say, "I bought those jeans with my own money" is wonderfully fulfilling. Whether you just want a little extra pocket money or you have something in mind that you're saving up for, learning a bit of financial responsibility is never a bad thing.

Learn Something New

All jobs will teach you something new. It might be something specific, like how to make a cappuccino or groom a poodle, or it will give you practice at soft skills, like how to work in a team or solve a problem with a customer. You might not use your poodle grooming skills again once you get a full-time adult job, but those soft skills will come in handy again and again.

Spend More Time Doing Something You Enjoy

If you have a hobby you love, like landscaping, drawing, or football, you could use a job as a way to turn this into something profitable. Coaching kids or helping out with a team you used to be a part of is a great way to get paid for doing something that you already enjoy. If it's something you want to be doing anyway, you might as well find a way to get paid!

Their Friends Have One

We've all done things because our friends did it first. It's not the worst reason to get a job, and a job has a lot more benefits than a nose ring, bangs, or any other trend you might have jumped on and ended up regretting. However, if you land an interview and can't drum up any enthusiasm, you're unlikely to end up with the job, so make sure you only go for things you will commit to. Be aware though: No matter how much fun it seems on TV, getting a job at the same place as your best friend is unlikely to end well.

Adults Insist on It!

Unfortunately, while you're a teenager, you still have to listen to what your carers say, and if they want you to spend less time napping and more time working, you'd better start working on your resume. From needing you to chip in with household finances to wanting to inspire you, adults have all sorts of reasons for asking you to get a job. You might resent it at first, but don't forget, you'll be learning valuable skills as well as pocketing some extra cash.

KEV CHILTON

Would You Like Fries With That?

Once you've worked out why you want a job, where should you start looking? Obviously you're not going to be taken on as a lawyer, doctor, or master builder straight away, I'm afraid first jobs tend to be limited to those where you don't need any prior skills, training, or experience. Because you're likely still be in school or college, you also don't want a job that expects you to be there full-time, so you're probably looking for something where you can work evenings or weekends.

The top industries for employing teenagers on a part-time basis are retail, hospitality, and janitorial—you're likely to be selling something, serving something, or cleaning something! These jobs are often referred to as unskilled jobs because they don't need a specific level of training or education in order to be able to carry them out.

Let's take a closer look at some of the specifics.

Retail

You might have noticed that shops are everywhere, so even if you move to the other end of the country for university, you'll probably be able to find another job in the same industry. What you're selling and who you're selling to might change, but the fundamentals of the job probably wont. Your duties are likely to entail working the cash register, finding items for customers, restocking shelves or clothes rails, tidying up, and sometimes even dealing with returns and complaints. If you're working in a small local store, you might get to know your regulars and start building a rapport, but if you're working for a large chain store, you'll probably serve hundreds of different people over the course of the week.

Some stores offer employee perks like discounts on their products or the chance to take home discontinued stock or food with a short shelf-life for free. It can be worth seeing if your favorite store is hiring or applying for places where you will use these benefits. Most retail positions are shift-based and you might work the same time each week or find yourself on a changing rota. Because the retail industry works seven days a week, and some stores are open late, you're likely to be able to get shifts that work around your school hours.

Benefits might include: employee discounts, weekend and evening shifts, transferable experience within the entire retail sector, and training given on the job.

Skills you need: friendly attitude, approachable, calm, polite (even if customers are rude to you), work in a team, good organization, and able to follow instructions.

Hospitality

KEV CHILTON

There's a lot more variety in hospitality because it covers everything from manning the drive-through at McDonalds to serving cocktails in a fivestar hotel. Again, the skills you learn in this industry can be used in jobs all over the country, and if you decide to turn your part-time job into a full-time career, there are lots of opportunities for development and progression. Employee discounts and free meals while you're on shift are popular ways of rewarding staff, and you can usually top up your wages with tips too.

Large cafes and restaurants usually split their staff into different teams, so you'll either be in the kitchen, behind the bar (if you're old enough), serving tables, greeting, or manning the register. This gives you a chance to get confident in one set of skills at a time. Smaller places might expect you to be more flexible, like taking orders and then making hot drinks and plating up pastries. Shifts can get busy around peak hours so be prepared to have to work fast, all while keeping a smile on your face.

Two of the easiest jobs for teens to start at are bussing tables (clearing away finished plates) and washing the dirty dishes. They're not glamorous jobs, but they're simple so you don't need a lot of training before you start. Waiting tables is another popular starting job and one that has more interaction with customers. Working as a barista in a coffee shop combines customer skills with being able to make all the drinks on the menu, and it's the starter job that takes the most training.

Benefits might include: employee discounts, evening and weekend shifts, on-the-job training, and a range of jobs to suit different people.

Skills you need: ability to work under pressure, polite and friendly attitude if dealing with customers, quick learner, and comfortable on your feet during a busy shift.

Janitorial

When offices, schools, and leisure centers close for the day, the cleaning crew is responsible for tidying up and getting them ready to open up in the morning. The hours are often late in the evening or early in the morning, so you need to be prepared to do a lot of your work when other people are sleeping, but the unsociable hours mean that these jobs often pay a little bit more for your trouble. You'll get all the equipment provided for you and a quick demonstration of how to use it, but that's all the training you'll need. Cleaners usually work in teams, so you'll have someone telling you which areas to work on, but then it's down to you.

If you don't like cleaning your room at home, this one might not be for you, but if the thought of vacuuming, emptying bins, and scrubbing toilets doesn't put you off, then this can be steady work. Day shift cleaners will work their way through a building while it's open, making sure that the toilets are stocked and there are no spillages in communal areas. Night shift cleaners don't have to worry about being seen by the public, making it a quiet and relaxed job. If you'd rather not have to deal with customers and are happy getting up early, this is an easy way to make money.

Benefits are: hours outside of school time, often leaving your weekends free, and no training needed.

Skills you need: an eye for detail and the ability to follow instructions and work on your own.

Apprenticeship vs Internship

If you're less interested in earning money and more focused on trying to get experience in a certain type of work, then one of these "ships" is going to suit you better. It can be a good idea to try out a field of work that you think you'll enjoy, especially if it's then going to influence what you study or where you train. Apprenticeships and internships might look the same on paper, but they work slightly differently.

Internships are fixed-term periods of work experience, usually lasting between 1-12 weeks. They aren't always paid positions and most are full-time, so it's best to apply for those that run outside of term time. As an intern, you'll be treated like any other employee and expected to dress, work, and behave like the rest of the staff. There's no better way to get an insight into the world of work than to actually try it out for yourself. However, internships are popular, especially those in industries like finance, publishing, and law, and you'll be up against more applicants than you would for a job at your local Starbucks.

Apprenticeships offer an alternative to staying at high school or going to university; instead, letting you work full-time while being paid and getting a qualification at the end of it. A lot of apprenticeships are in physical jobs like construction, plumbing, sports coaching, or forestry, where academic qualifications are less important than practical skills. The program will last for at least a year and you'll have some study to do alongside the hours you work, but you'll be building important skills that can lead you to a full-time job as an adult.

Both internships and apprenticeships have application processes to follow and might state minimum levels of arithmetic and English skills needed. You can get information from your school's career advisor or by searching online. Take your time to read all the information given to make sure you are eligible and you understand what you need to do next.

KEV CHILTON

Going It Alone

Getting your first employed job can be difficult, especially if there are a lot of teens your age who are also looking. If you don't have any experience, you might end up missing out, but how can you get experience if no one will hire you? It's the eternal job-hunting paradox, but there is a solution: work for yourself.

Some teens find ways to earn money by being self-employed. All that means is you are in charge of finding work and providing a service to a good standard, and it's a nice fancy way of lumping together all the jobs like babysitting, mowing the lawn, walking your neighbor's dog, and anything else you might do and be paid for. Self-employed work lets you use your existing skills and pursue particular areas of interest. If you have a talent, like playing an instrument or sketching portraits, you could try and find ways to make money by performing or taking commissions.

The downside to being self-employed is that the money probably isn't regular, especially when you're starting out. You also have to put in some work marketing yourself, which means putting up flyers, posting them in mailboxes, or knocking door to door around the neighborhood and introducing yourself. Don't be afraid to ask people to recommend you or to use friends and family to find work. For example, if you regularly babysit for your

TEENS' GUIDE TO FINANCIAL INDEPENDENCE

Aunt, ask her to see if any of her friends or colleagues are looking for a new sitter.

Here are some of the top self-employed jobs that you could think about getting into:

- Babysitting. If you love kids and have experience with little ones, this is probably the easiest way to make some extra money. Having your own car is a plus, but some families are happy to drive their sitter home at the end of the night. As an added bonus, once you put the kids to bed, you're then getting paid to do your homework or watch TV!

- Pet sitting or walking. Popping around to feed your neighbor's cat while they're on holiday won't make you a millionaire overnight, but you can charge a little more if you also water plants, collect the mail, and give the house a quick clean before they return. Dog walkers can charge an hourly rate, as those pups need regular exercise, so you can quickly build up a solid client base.

- Gardening. Usually you'll be mowing lawns, but some customers might need help with other jobs like trimming hedges, weeding flowerbeds, and raking up leaves. You need to be physically fit, especially if you do a few houses in the same day, but people are usually willing to pay a good rate for someone to take care of jobs they can't or don't want to do.

- Tutoring. If you're strong in academic subjects, you can make money tutoring those in the years below you, especially if they have important exams coming up that they need help with. Tutoring in a musical instrument is also popular, especially if you play locally and are well-known.

- Car washing—another job that people don't always like doing themselves. You can charge per car and if you put the effort into marketing yourself well, you could get the whole street buying your services. All you need to invest in is a bucket, some sponges, car wash fluid, and a good set of overalls.

- Sports refereeing. Local Sunday league teams might not play in the big leagues, but they still need referees and umpires to make sure the kids stick to the rules. If you have a passion for a certain sport, it's worth looking into getting qualified as an official. Although you'll have to pay to take a course, you'll make that money back in no time. You don't have to be affiliated with a particular club and you can take on as many matches as you feel able to.

If You Can't Get Paid, Get Experience

TEENS' GUIDE TO FINANCIAL INDEPENDENCE

Remember that paradox I mentioned earlier? Here's another way around it. If you're really struggling to get a job because they always hire someone who already has experience, why not get the experience by volunteering? Okay, you won't get paid for it, but you will still gain those wonderful soft skills, as well as making yourself much more appealing for the next paid job you apply for.

There are hundreds of different organizations that rely on volunteers to provide services within the community. Volunteering your time is rewarding, and it also helps you build your self-confidence. Charity shops and thrift stores rely on volunteer cashiers and stock workers so that most of their profits can go to good causes, and in return, they can train you in making sales and interacting with customers. Hospitals and care homes employ volunteers to help with admin and to interact with patients and visitors, providing insight into the workings of the healthcare sector. Animal shelters need volunteers to feed the animals and socialize them, helping them to get homes and giving you an excuse to play fetch with Fido.

If you're interested in volunteering opportunities near you, check out the websites for your local charities and see if they have anything listed. Your school or college might be able to put you in touch with organizations that regularly take on student volunteers, or you can search through national programs and initiatives.

KEV CHILTON

Chapter Two

How to Sell Yourself

When you are asked if you can do a job, tell 'em, 'Certainly I can!' Then get busy and find out how to do it.
–Theodore Roosevelt

The process of applying for a job is pretty standard these days: You see an advert for a position and you reply with a copy of your resume and sometimes a cover letter explaining why you want the job. Sometimes, especially for unskilled jobs, there is an application form to fill in instead of providing your resume. This makes it easier for employers to compare all the applicants, and it's also easier for you because you don't have to worry about missing something important on your resume.

Building up your self-employed business is a little different. You might respond to an advert from someone looking for a helper, but they will probably be much more interested in speaking to you than reading your resume. If you're trying to find more customers, you might write your own flyer or advert, in which you can showcase your skills and experience in a less formal way. It will have much of the same information as a resume and its function is still to sell you to someone who will pay for your services.

If you've never written a resume before, you might wonder where to start. You can ask your school career advisor if they have any examples to show you, or you can look online at some templates, but these are often a lot more detailed than you'll need for a part-time job. In this section, I'm going to walk you through what information to include on your resume and show you that you're a lot more experienced and qualified than you think. Then, after each section, I'll include some model answers from some of the teens in my life so you can see what some of your peers included in their resumes.

Your Best Qualities

In the previous chapter, I mentioned something called soft skills. You might have heard these mentioned at school or by other adults, but if they haven't explained exactly what they are, you might be left a little in the dark. Hard skills are easier to define. Having a hard skill means you are able to do something, like perform CPR, drive a car safely, cook a casserole, or speak another language fluently. Soft skills show your awareness of a situation and your ability to respond to people and tasks in a sensitive and productive manner. Can you work in a team successfully, learn from mistakes, and show common sense? Soft skills help you to navigate life and the workplace, and they're often looked at by employers as more important than qualifications. This is because hard skills are easier to teach, so if you don't know how to operate the photocopier in the office, you can learn by reading the manual or asking someone else. But if you don't have the common sense to do either of those things, and instead end up jamming the paper and breaking the machine, you can cause a lot of problems.

This should be good news for you, because you will have many wonderful soft skills but not much work experience or training. If you can show your soft skills on your resume or in your advert, you will make yourself very attractive to prospective employers and customers. You just need to work out what soft skills you actually have, so let's have a look at some examples that are highly valued in the workplace.

- Good time management. You're on time, or early, for work and can do the tasks you're given quickly and well.

- Trustworthy and reliable. You do what is expected every time, and you won't do anything that would be bad for the business, like post negative comments on social media or steal from the register.

- Good manners. You are polite when speaking to customers and other employees, keep your area tidy, and offer to help others when you can.

- Self-motivation You want to improve your skills and experience and take the initiative to look for ways to perform better at your job.

- Positive attitude. You come to work ready to do your job and don't complain about your shift duties or bad-mouth the customers and other employees.

- Good communication skills. You are able to explain policies and processes and be understood by both employees and customers.

Did you read through the list and recognize yourself in some of those descriptions? The soft skills needed to succeed at school are also the soft skills that are really important in the workplace, so as long as you can identify your strong points, you should have plenty to talk about on your resume. Just like Ben and Maia:

TEENS' GUIDE TO FINANCIAL INDEPENDENCE

Ben has been asked to babysit his neighbor's five-year-old son a couple of times and has decided to try and see if he can get some more families to hire him. He's putting together a flyer to post to the other houses on his street. He's identified that being trustworthy and reliable is important to parents, as well as good time management and being friendly and fun.

Abby needs to get a job so that she can save up enough to pay the insurance when she starts driving her Dad's car. There are lots of places hiring in her local town because they need extra staff for the Christmas season, but she knows she needs to stand out. She wants to show that she's motivated to succeed and has good communication skills. She also thinks it's important to highlight her confidence and ability to use her initiative.

Quiz Time

If you're still not sure what soft skills you have, here is a quick quiz to help you discover a couple of them. Choose the answer that most closely fits with how true the given statement is. At the end of each section, check the key and add up your points to see what your soft skills are and what type of job these would benefit.

People Skills

KEV CHILTON

		Always	Often	Sometimes	Never
A	I listen when other people talk to me.				
B	If I'm shouted at for something I haven't done, I stay calm and explain the mistake.				
C	Talking to people tires me out.				
D	People find it difficult to follow what I tell them.				
E	I can tell how someone is feeling when they talk to me.				

Key

- **A:** 3, 2, 1, 0 points
- **B:** 3, 2, 1, 0 points
- **C:** 0, 1, 2, 3 points
- **D:** 0, 1, 2, 3, points
- **E:** 3, 2, 1, 0 points

If you scored 10+ points, you have strong communication skills that will help you when working with customers.

TEENS' GUIDE TO FINANCIAL INDEPENDENCE

If you scored 7–9 points, you have some good communication skills but there's room for improvement.

If you scored 6 or less, good communication is probably not one of your strong points, so you might want to look for a job that isn't going to have you speaking to customers for the whole shift.

Time Management

		Always	Often	Sometimes	Never
A	I plan my journeys so that I arrive early.				
B	Teachers have to chase me for my school assignments.				
C	If someone asks me to do something while I'm busy, I let them know when I'll be able to start.				
D	I feel like there aren't enough hours in the day for everything I have to do.				
E	I do my homework as soon as it is set.				

Key

KEV CHILTON

- **A:** 3, 2, 1, 0 points
- **B:** 0, 1, 2, 3 points
- **C:** 3, 2, 1, 0 points
- **D:** 0, 1, 2, 3, points
- **E:** 3, 2, 1, 0 points

If you scored 10+ points, you are great at managing your time effectively, making you someone employers can rely on to get the job done on time.

If you scored 7–9 points, you are reasonably good with time management but might struggle to manage lots of tasks if you need to prioritize them.

If you scored 6 or less, your time management skills need to improve, which will make you feel less stressed and rushed and make you more reliable.

Attitude

TEENS' GUIDE TO FINANCIAL INDEPENDENCE

		Always	Often	Sometimes	Never
A	When someone calls me I assume something bad has happened.				
B	Once I'm having a bad day, nothing can cheer me up.				
C	I try to see the best in every situation.				
D	Seeing other people happy makes me happy.				
E	I try and have a good day, every day.				

Key

A: 0, 1, 2, 3 points

B: 0, 1, 2, 3 points

C: 3, 2, 1, 0 points

D: 3, 2, 1, 0 points

E: 3, 2, 1, 0 points

If you scored 10+ points, you have a positive attitude and always look on the bright side. This can rub off on customers and help to diffuse situations where they are unhappy.

KEV CHILTON

If you scored 7–9 points, you have good days and bad days, which is pretty normal for a teenager! Work on making sure your bad mood doesn't make you grumpy in front of customers and you'll be fine.

If you scored 6 or less, your attitude can be negatively affected by a lot of things in your life, so make sure you're looking after yourself. You might feel more comfortable in a job that isn't customer-facing.

Motivation

		Always	Often	Sometimes	Never
A	I find it easy to get out of bed in the morning.				
B	Given the choice between an easy and a hard task, I like to challenge myself with the hard one.				
C	I'm okay with not being the best all the time.				
D	I only put effort into something if I'm passionate about it.				
E	Doing something I don't like is worth it if there's a reward at the end.				

TEENS' GUIDE TO FINANCIAL INDEPENDENCE

Key

A: 3, 2, 1, 0 points

B: 3, 2, 1, 0 points

C: 0, 1, 2, 3 points

D: 0, 1, 2, 3, points

E: 3, 2, 1, 0 points

If you scored 10+ points, you are motivated to make the best of yourself and enjoy the challenge of improving.

If you scored 7-9 points, you are reasonably good with motivating yourself but might struggle if you have a hard day.

If you scored 6 or less, you are probably more motivated by enjoyment than achievement. A job where you can indulge a passion or hobby is going to bring the best out of you.

What Counts as Experience?

In chapter one, I said that one of the biggest hurdles teens face when trying to get their first job is that they don't have any experience. The thing is, you actually have lots of really valuable and relevant experience; you just have to work a bit harder to show it. You might not have worked in a café before, but you've probably made food, plated it up for siblings, washed the dishes, and cleaned the kitchen when you're done. All these life experiences can be included somewhere in your resume or cover letter.

Your first resume won't have that much information on it, whereas mine easily fills two pages. This might sound like a bad thing, but actually, it gives you lots of space to include hobbies and extracurricular activities that can help you get the job. Do you have something you do regularly, like play a team sport or take a class outside of school? Congratulations! This shows you have commitment and dedication—more valuable soft skills that employers are looking for. If you always stay behind after practice to tidy up or have taken it upon yourself to organize who brings study group refreshments, mention that too, because it shows you have initiative and are a team player.

When employers look through resumes, it's easy for them to assume everyone comes from the same background, family situation, and opportunities. If you take on extra responsibilities at home, put those in your resume. Anything from walking the dog to caring for relatives is important experience and shows off your soft skills. Employers want someone who is reliable—who can be trusted to do an important job—so the fact that your caregivers give you the responsibility to look after others when they can't says a lot about your character, and if you've had to step up at home because no one else is, that says even more. Here's what Ben and Maia identified as useful experience for their resumes.

Abby is a prefect at school and runs a weekly reading group for younger children. She puts this on her resume to show that she is organized and reliable. She also mentions that she goes to the care home every Sunday afternoon, the only day her Dad can't visit, because she knows how much her Grandma enjoys getting visitors. She wants employers to see that she is caring and puts other people first. She decides not to include the fact that she is the only one at home who ever remembers to feed the hamster because she thinks it will sound trivial.

Ben starts his flyer with a paragraph introducing himself. He has been on the school soccer team for three years and hardly ever misses practice. He lists the awards the team has won and the big competitions he has been a part of, because he wants to show that he has commitment and doesn't let down his team when they rely on him. He also adds that he helps coach the younger teams, adding more experience to show that he is good with small children. He already has babysitting experience, so he makes sure that's highlighted somewhere on the page.

Putting Together Your First Resume

KEV CHILTON

Now that we've had a little look at some of the content you can put on your resume, we need to start putting everything together. Your skills and experience are probably the most important pieces of information you can add, but you need to include some other bits as standard. Every resume should include:

- your name, address, phone number and email address,

- a personal statement summing up all your strengths in a couple of sentences

- those soft skills you've been working on identifying

- the name of your school or college and any qualifications or grades achieved or predicted so far

- work experience, if you have any. Some schools ask their students to organize mandatory work experience placements, so if you did this, don't forget to include it.

- appropriate hobbies and interests (going shopping and eating pizza don't count, I'm afraid), including teams or groups you are a part of, competitions you have entered, if you have a significant online following (you post guitar lessons on YouTube, for example), and any volunteering you have undertaken.

You can mess around slightly with the order, especially if you download some templates that use sidebars and section boxes, but the general rule of thumb is that the most important qualities should come first. Employers will probably be looking through hundreds of resumes, especially for retail and hospitality jobs, and after a while, they all start to look the same. You need to make sure they can easily see your name, contact details, and your key skills. If the key skills you've listed aren't right for the role, they might not keep reading to discover that you're the top student in your year and you volunteer to read to cats every weekend.

Getting Personal

The only thing that's new on that list is a personal statement. Imagine it like your dating profile for jobs. It should let them know your strengths, values, and experience, as well as why you would be a good fit for the job. I know that sounds like a lot to fit into a couple of sentences, but you'll be surprised how simple it is once you highlight the key points. Blurbs on the back of books manage to sell you on the story in just a few paragraphs, and the Netflix descriptions of movies and TV shows do the same with only a sentence. I know the personal statement comes near the beginning of your resume, but if you write it last, you'll have an easier time summarizing the key points. Start by stating clearly who you are, like so:

[One or two adjectives to describe you] high school/college student with [most recent exams or grades].

Use words like motivated, responsible, high-achieving, and other positive terms. If you have your driving license you could tag this information on the end, as being able to get around by yourself might make you more appealing.

Then, move on to any experience you already have, either from work, volunteering, school, or hobbies. Explicitly mention how these demonstrate your soft skills or are relevant to the job. Here's another example:

Dedicated member of the athletics club for three years, twice county finalist, and school librarian, responsible for restocking returned books, recommending reads, and keeping the library tidy.

This shows that you are committed and loyal, you have a drive to do well, and you have some basic customer service and shelving skills. Let's look at another example:

I love cooking and regularly plan and prepare healthy meals for my family. I am also responsible for collecting my younger sisters from school and making sure they do their homework on time.

TEENS' GUIDE TO FINANCIAL INDEPENDENCE

This simple statement shows you are responsible and trustworthy, (presumably) good with kids, and have been motivated to learn some cooking and nutrition skills.

The final sentence of your personal statement should explain why you want this particular job. Obviously, you can't just put that you need money, but the employers who are looking at hiring teenagers won't be expecting you to have dreamed of being a waitress since you were small. All you need to do is try and tie your existing skills to the demands of the role and show that you've thought about what the job entails, not just blindly applied for anything and everything.

Looking for a [type of job (e.g.: in sales, kitchen, or cleaning)] that allows me to build on my [relevant skills] and develop my [skill you'd like to learn or improve].

If you're applying for different kinds of jobs you should keep multiple copies of your resume, each with a slightly different personal statement that is relevant to the industry you're looking at. What you write for a job washing dishes will look different than what you write for a job as a cashier because the two roles have different key skills.

To give you some more examples, here's Ben's flyer and Abby's finished resume.

Ben

KEV CHILTON

Because Ben is advertising directly to customers, he doesn't have a formal resume. He writes a flyer and places his personal statement directly under the title. Then he puts his experience and skills on one side of the page and writes a warm and positive paragraph about himself on the other. He puts his contact details at the bottom. He has also asked his neighbors if they'll recommend him, and they've written a statement that he's included under his personal statement.

<u>Need A Sitter?</u>

I am a friendly and experienced high school student who has been babysitting for six months. I coach junior soccer in my spare time and I have experience with children from age 5–12. I'm responsible, always on time, and happy to help with homework and cooking dinner if needed.

<u>Key Skills:</u>

- trustworthy
- reliable
- fun-loving and easy-going
- good with children
- basic cooking skills
- predicted top grades in all core subjects

TEENS' GUIDE TO FINANCIAL INDEPENDENCE

<u>About Me</u>

Hi, my name is Ben and I live at 25 Sycamore Drive. I really enjoy working with children and am thinking of studying to be a teacher when I'm older. I love soccer and I've been on the school team for three years now. We made it to the county finals last year and I was voted best defender by my coaches. I also help to coach the Fartown Flyers junior team. The kids love me, and I really enjoy teaching them new skills and watching how excited they get when they play.

I started babysitting six months ago, and I find it a really rewarding job. I like to ask the kids what they want to do for the evening and enjoy learning about their interests. I'm game for anything, as long as its within the rules, and I'll always follow your instructions about screen time, snacks, homework, bedtime, and anything else you think I need to know.

If you would like to meet me, please send me a message and we can arrange a time.

<u>Reference</u>

Eli loves it when Ben comes to sit; it makes it really easy to leave the house guilt-free! The house is always tidy when we get back and Eli tells me they usually watch a movie or play with his Legos. I'd definitely recommend Ben to anyone looking for some more child-free time! -Sandy, no. 21.

Abby

After looking at all the jobs advertised at the mall, Abby has decided she'd rather work in the retail stores than the cafés or fast food restaurants. She tailors her resume and personal statement to reflect that she's comfortable dealing with people and solving problems.

Personal Statement

Driven and successful high school prefect with excellent predicted grades. Used my initiative to start a weekly book club for students and help pair them up with older tutors to help their grades. Looking for a sales job that allows me to build on my excellent communication and problem-solving skills and develop my customer service experience.

Key Skills:

- I'm confident and always willing to try new things.
- I'm punctual and good at planning my time to make sure I get everything done.
- I'm reliable and trustworthy as demonstrated by the responsibilities I have been given at school.

- I'm good at solving problems, thinking outside the box, and using my initiative.

- I'm an effective communicator and diplomatic when dealing with people who are upset.

Experience

I organize and run a weekly book club and study group at school. We vote on books to read and make sure we choose a variety so we can appeal to people of all interests and abilities. Last year some of the younger students approached me and said they were really enjoying the club and wondered if I would help tutor them in English as they were struggling. I recruited some other pupils from my year and we matched every older pupil to a couple of younger students and I spoke to the staff about booking a study room every week.

On Sundays, I visit my Grandad in the nursing home for a couple of hours and help the staff out with some duties like cleaning his room and making tea for the residents. Sometimes I will organize an activity in the break room, like a game of Scrabble or a jigsaw competition, especially if the staff are very busy.

Hobbies and Interests

I love reading and writing and have had a couple of poems published in online competitions. Last year I took a

KEV CHILTON

summer writing course because I wanted to improve my technique.

I'm about to start learning to drive, and I want to be able to travel more once I have my license. I enjoy hiking and camping and would love to take a tour of the lakes where I can go wild swimming.

Chapter Three

Interview Techniques

Success is walking from failure to failure with no loss of enthusiasm. –Winston Churchill

Once you've created your resume, you can either use it directly to apply for jobs or use it as the template when you fill out an application form. If your skills, experience, and personal qualities match what they're looking for, an employer will contact you and invite you to come for an interview. It's worth mentioning at this point that how you speak on this call can also be considered a pre-interview, so make sure you're polite and thank them for giving you the opportunity.

You'll be given a time and place to have the interview. This will usually be at the store, restaurant, office, or other place of work where you have applied; however, it could also be at a neutral venue, like the coffee shop next door. Some interviews are done over video call, so make sure you have a good internet connection and a private room where you can talk without being interrupted. It's a good idea to have a backup laptop or phone on hand in case anything goes wrong. It should not be at a private residence, so if you are offered an interview at the manager's house, something isn't right and you should politely decline. The exception to this is if you are interviewing for a business run out of someone's home—for example, a cleaning or dog-walking business—or you are self-employed and have been invited by a prospective new client.

During your interview, the employer will ask you questions to assess your suitability for the role. Most of the time, they ask the same sort of questions, which is great because it means you can practice beforehand and work on some planned answers.

Typical interview questions include:

- Can you tell me something about yourself? This is the personal statement of the interview, so make sure you mention all your wonderful skills and the interesting things you've done.

- Can you tell me about a time when you had to work under pressure? Other examples include: overcoming a challenge, working as a team, and showing initiative. It's important to have thought of a few examples beforehand so you can show how you used your skills to deal with a problem.

- What are your strengths and weaknesses? Your strengths should be easy because we've already covered your top skills, but thinking of weaknesses is harder. They don't want to hear that you are always late to places or you're pretty clumsy and always drop things. Choose something that you can put a positive spin on, like "I can be too hard on myself because I have high expectations" or "I tend to put others first, which means I can say yes to helping out instead of doing things I wanted."

- What shifts are you available for? It can be tempting to say, "all of them," but it's best to be realistic. If you have regular commitments, mention them at the interview. Unless the job advert specified hours, you and the employer should be able to work out a schedule that benefits you both. Don't promise more hours than you can manage or you'll end up being unreliable and your schoolwork might suffer.

- Have you got any questions for us? Make sure you have questions for them too, as it shows you're really interested in what the job would be like. You could ask what a typical shift might look like, how the employees would describe the team, if there are any employee benefits not listed in the advert, or what your manager would love you to be doing in one week, month, and year from your start date.

If you are being interviewed by a prospective client for a self-employed job like garden maintenance or babysitting, your interview chat will be a lot more formal. It should be a mix of them asking questions about you and you showing an interest in them and their job. Ask about what hours they were thinking of, discuss the needs of their child/pet, or if anything in their garden or house needs special care. Remember to be friendly and confident.

Tips and Tricks

Practice interviews with your friends, family, school teachers, or even just yourself in the mirror. The more comfortable you can be answering questions about yourself, the better you will come across in an actual interview.

Research the company and find out some information that you can drop into the conversation. This shows that you've taken the time to apply for this specific job, not just any job out there. You could express your excitement at their new menu items, praise their ethical manufacturing, or just say that you like how thoughtfully their stores are laid out.

End your answers with questions for the interviewer. This can be a way of leading on to the next topic you want to talk about so you can feel a bit more in control. This is easier to do if your interviewer isn't just working their way through a list of questions.

Even if you're interviewing for a night cleaning job where you'll work alone and in overalls, you should wear something smart and presentable for the interview. Avoid anything that reveals excess skin (i.e.: crop tops, tank tops, strappy tops, mini skirts, hot pants) and anything with funny or offensive images. Chinos or a knee-length skirt and a plain shirt, t-shirt, or polo shirt will help you look presentable. Ignore all of this if you're interviewing for somewhere with a specific niche look, like a 1950s diner or a metal music store—if this is the case, wear something that shows you can pull off the right look.

Think about how your body language represents you as well as the answers you give. Sit up straight and make eye contact with the interviewer when they're asking you a question and when you give your reply. If there are multiple interviewers, you should direct your answer to the person who asked the questions, but you don't have to stare at them the whole time. Even if you're nervous—and why wouldn't you be? Interviews scared

KEV CHILTON

the life out of me even after forty years—try and smile, especially at the start when greeting everyone.

Don't be afraid to slow things down. If they ask you a question, it's okay to ask for a minute to think about the answer; you don't need to have it on the top of your tongue already. I've interviewed some people who started talking before they knew what they wanted to say, and I could always tell the moment their thoughts caught up with their words! Anything before then was just rambling.

Despite my reputation as a skilled interviewer, I always felt intimidated when I had to be the one answering questions. One day, after another disastrous interview where I was rejected for a position I really wanted, one of the interviewers reached out to me. He recognized that my potential was being stifled in the interview process and offered to help. He suggested that I make an appointment with his secretary and he would give me 20 minutes of his time. Those 20 minutes turned out to be the most valuable anyone has ever given me.

I scheduled an appointment for interview coaching, but it didn't go as I had expected. To my surprise, this senior police officer bluntly told me, "Kev, you're terrible at interviews." Feeling completely defeated, he then shared with me how I could salvage my next interview if it followed the same pattern as my previous ones. He advised me to memorize a specific phrase that would, at the very least, give me a fighting chance. Typically, at the end of an interview, you have the chance to make a closing statement. This is where you really shine. These words may not seem like much on paper, but when spoken with genuine emotion, they work like magic:

Firstly, I'd like to thank you for giving me the opportunity of this interview, and secondly, I want you to know that I applied for this position because I wanted it, and if I were successful today, you will get my very best, and I won't let you down.

Now, let's look deeper into this. You might think the first part is unnecessary, but it's actually quite important. It portrays you as a polite individual and, most importantly, it conveys your genuine desire for the job. It may sound strange, but in the hiring process, interviewers often encounter candidates who aren't particularly invested in the outcome. Yes, it's bizarre, but many people apply for numerous jobs with the hope of landing anything they can. Interview panels are aware of this, so you need to distinguish yourself from those who aren't as interested... and by doing so, you automatically rise above them in the ranking. Great first move on your part!

Next comes the confirmation of your commitment to the interviewers. By emphasizing your future loyalty to them, it's like music to their ears. They don't want the embarrassment of selecting someone who won't perform well because if they make the wrong choice, it reflects poorly on them too. And here's the best part. If you learn to articulate these words clearly, concisely, and convincingly, they will stick in their minds and be the first thing they remember when reviewing their interview notes and deciding whom to hire.

Trust me, I've had some very unexceptional interviews and still managed to secure positions I never should have, all because of these words!

Interviewing Prospective Clients

When you're working for yourself, interviews tend to look a little different. They're more of a conversation between you and the people thinking about hiring you. They will have things they want to ask, but you will have a lot of questions too because this interview didn't come with a job advert so you want to know their expectations. As you'll probably be working in their home or with their children or pets, they'll want to get to know you and possibly even see you in action.

These interviews are considerably less formal. You might chat over the phone or you might meet at their house. Be prepared to explain what your work will look like, rather than asking about a shift pattern. For example, a friend of mine tutors kids after school and she still has these kinds of informal interviews. She will chat for a little bit about the school and what the children like and then talk the parents through what her lessons will look like and how she works. The reason she starts by connecting with the kids is because personal relationships are very important in her job, and if they don't get along then the kids don't improve as fast. If you're looking for babysitting work, then you won't go wrong with a similar approach.

Here are a few other examples to show how you might pitch your work to potential clients:

- Gardening: Feel free to show up in your overalls or something casual. Compliment their garden and mention a favorite feature. Give them a quick rundown of some of the services you offer (e.g.: mowing the lawn, pruning plants, trimming hedges, or watering plant pots), and show them photos of things you've done before. Ask what they are looking for, discuss how often you'll visit, and then give them your price. Don't forget to mention if you'll bring your own tools or if you need to borrow theirs.

- Babysitting: Start by asking all about their children, what they like and what their routine is. Ask whether they're looking for regular or occasional care and let them know how much you charge per hour. Make sure you let them know if there are times when you can't work. Talk about your previous experience, if you have any, and mention some interests you have that can make things fun for their kids (e.g.: you could bring your guitar and sing songs, or you love painting and crafting). Spend some time interacting with their child so the parents can see how you get along.

- Dog-walking or pet-sitting: Let the owners know what you offer (e.g.: group or solo walks, in-home care, how often you can visit) and if you have experience with their type of animal. Don't forget to let them know what each option costs. Find out if they have a specific regular schedule in mind (like a walk before and after school) or if they want someone just for when they're away. Go through any rules you have, like only walking the dog on the lead, and make sure they're okay with them. Ask if they have any specific rules or things you need to know, if their pet has an allergy, and what commands they know. Obviously, you need to ask to meet the pet and, if you're offering a walking service, maybe agree to go on one together so they can see how you treat their fur baby.

- Music Lessons: Bring your instrument (if you can) or ask to use theirs if it's large. Demonstrate how you play and then get them, or their kid, to have a go. Give them the prices for your lessons and explain if you want them to commit to a certain number upfront. Discuss a time that suits you both and talk to them about your expectations for practicing outside of lesson times. Ask if there's a particular style of music that they would like to focus on. Make sure they know if you charge extra for providing sheet music or if you need them to buy their own.

Getting Back Out There

Very few people apply for one job, have one interview, and get offered the position. You might have to send out twenty resumes to get five interviews and do all five before you get one offer. Rejection is part of the experience, but you mustn't take it personally. If you get an interview, it means you had the right skills to do the job; celebrate this and be encouraged to apply for similar jobs. If you didn't get an interview, review your resume and see if there's anything you'd like to change.

Rejection after an interview can feel personal, but at that stage, most employers are looking for the right person to fit into an existing team, and it might be that they didn't feel you'd gel with the rest of the staff. Don't be afraid to ask for feedback so that you can know what worked well at your interview and what was seen as a turn-off.

KEV CHILTON

Practice makes perfect, so take your feedback and use it to improve for the next time.

If you've had several interviews without success, you could ask a trusted adult to go over your interview technique with you and see if they can give you some tips. Most of the adults you know will have had to go through a lot of job interviews, both for new roles and promotions, and they have a wealth of experience that I'm sure they'd be delighted to pass on. You know adults love nothing better than giving advice, right?

Chapter Four

What Do I Do Now That I'm Here?

WHENEVER THINGS GO A bit sour in a job I'm doing, I always tell myself, you can do better than this. –Dr. Seuss

Congratulations! Your interview was successful and you've been offered your first job. You're about to venture into a whole new chapter in your life and experience something brand new. It's like you've unlocked a new area in a video game or started watching a spin-off of your favorite show. The workplace has its own set of rules, its own characters, and its own problems, and no matter how much the adults in your life have told you that school will prepare you for work, it really won't.

One of the biggest differences between school and work is that you probably won't get the same level of support if things start to go wrong. If you don't put the effort in at school, teachers will give you extra sessions or set up tutoring groups to make sure you can still succeed, but if you don't try at work, you'll probably just end up losing the job. Depending on the type of work and the expectations of the company, you might be given some retraining or be put on a performance management plan where you're given targets to improve, but don't count on someone jumping in to help you. Employees are expected to be independent and responsible for their own success.

Expected Behavior and Consequences

When you start a new job, you should be given a contract and an employee manual. The contract should be signed by both you and the employer, as it states your legal rights while you're working there. You should read it carefully before signing it and make sure you ask questions if there's anything you don't understand. At a minimum, your contract should include the following information:

1. Your job title and a description of the work. This will include the hours you're required to work and whether they are fixed or subject to change. It should also say where you work and what the key duties of your role are.

2. Your pay and other benefits, including if there are

any deductions for tax, insurance, health care, and your pension. This should also include information about holiday pay and how many vacation days you can take.

3. The process of termination and how it works if you decide to quit or you are fired. It's important to know how long your notice period is and what information the company has to provide you with if they decide they don't want you to work there anymore.

Your employee manual is like a textbook for work: It will tell you everything you need to know about your job, how you're expected to behave, and who you can talk to if you have a complaint. Even if you've worked or volunteered in a similar job before, you should read the handbook carefully because it will have specific expectations for this role, and if you miss something important you might find yourself in trouble.

For any job where you will be interacting with customers, working as part of a team, or using equipment provided by the employer, there will be general rules you'll need to follow, and now that you have some idea of what to expect, I'll explain some of them here.

Basic Expectations

KEV CHILTON

Different workplaces will have different rules on how they want you to dress—for example, clothing stores might prefer their employees to only wear their own brand while working—but if there isn't a uniform, a general rule is to wear something smart casual. You need to be comfortable but also look respectable. Pop into the store before you start working, see what the other employees are wearing, and make sure you find something similar.

Workplaces are getting more tolerant about employing people with visible tattoos, piercings, and unnatural hair coloring, but you will still find restrictions in some places. Make sure you check what is permitted, especially if you're thinking about changing your look once you're already employed.

Don't take your phone or wear your smartwatch while you're working. If you have a secure staffroom or a locker, leave it in there, otherwise leave it in the car or at home. Your employer won't be happy if you're caught checking your messages during your shift, especially if it's in front of customers. If there's an important reason why you need to have your phone on you, make sure you clear it with your manager first.

One of the lovely things about having a job is getting to make new friends with people who work on your team, but this doesn't mean you can stand around chatting all day. Some people get distracted from their work by talking to others, so even if that's not you, it's not fair to others if you can multitask and they can't. Also, if you're supposed to be ringing up customers, it's very rude to ignore them and talk to your colleagues instead. Save the chatting for break times and after work.

Not all jobs involve dealing with customers, but if your role does, you need to make sure you're always friendly and polite, even if you're having a bad day yourself. It's one of the hardest things about customer-facing roles, and you should think carefully about whether they're right for you before you apply for one. Customers can be rude, frustrating, and ignorant, but you still have to smile at them and help them with their problems. Being rude to a customer is one of the top reasons why you can get fired from your job.

Just like at school, you're probably not going to be best friends with everyone you work with. It's tough luck if you get paired on a shift with someone you don't like, but you need to ignore your differences while you're at work and remember that you're both part of a team and that means you need to work together. Being rude or unhelpful to your colleagues might mean they put in a complaint about you.

It's important that you are reliable at work and that means turning up on time for every shift. You need to manage your journey there and back to account for traffic problems and late buses, because these excuses will wear thin very quickly. If you can't make a shift, you should let your manager know as soon as possible, or arrange to swap with someone else if that's policy.

Getting It Wrong

Be aware that many jobs have a probationary period for the first few months where you are given a chance to settle into the role, but if things aren't working out during this time, your manager can let you go much more easily. After this, if your behavior at work doesn't meet the expectations of your manager, you will probably be called in for a performance management meeting. They will discuss any issues with you, such as complaints from other team members or customers, records of mistakes or problems with your behavior, or your ability to perform the duties of your role. If they want to keep you on and help you improve, your manager will set out some targets for you, give you a reasonable time to meet them, and explain how they're going to support you to do so.

It can feel awful to be called for a performance management meeting, so if this happens to you, take a couple of days to process the information and your emotions. Then prepare yourself for your next shift and make sure you take working toward your targets seriously. If you don't show improvement by your next scheduled meeting, you may not be given another chance.

Responsibilities and Duties

Once you have a job, you have certain tasks you are responsible for during your shift. These would have been in the job description, mentioned at the interview, and also laid out in your contract and employee manual. For example, someone working in a supermarket could be expected to work the cash register, restock shelves at the end of the shift, clean up any spillages, and help customers find items in the store.

Your job probably has a long list of duties, but you won't be expected to do them all at once and they will change depending on where you've been asked to work each shift. One day, you might be unpacking deliveries and organizing the stockroom, and the next shift, you're helping customers find a jacket that fits. While you can be asked to do anything that's reasonably part of your job, you should always know what your employer cannot ask you to do. Here are some examples:

- There should be a maximum number of hours you can work in a week, a shift, and without a break. You'll need to check your local labor laws to find out what these are. In many places, it's 40 hours a week, 8 hours a shift, and 4 hours without a break.

- You should not usually be asked to work overnight, unless this is a specific part of your job (e.g.: You work in a bar or as an early morning cleaner). You should also have a break of at least 8 hours where you can sleep, so between 10 p.m. and 6 a.m. or 11 p.m. and 7 a.m.

- Your employer must not ask you to do anything you aren't trained for, if the activity requires a specific qualification. So, you can't handle hazardous waste or operate a forklift truck, even if they get someone to supervise you.

- You can't be asked to do work that you're unable to do, either physically or mentally, and it can't be held against you if you refuse. This might include lifting heavy boxes in a warehouse or cold-calling people if you suffer from anxiety.

- You shouldn't be asked to work so much that it impacts your studies. From time to time, you might be given extra shifts or asked to cover for someone who is unwell, but regular hours that mean you are too tired for school and don't get time to rest and relax aren't good for you, even if you need the money.

TEENS' GUIDE TO FINANCIAL INDEPENDENCE

Sometimes your employer might ask you to work longer or later because there's an emergency, and if you feel safe and comfortable saying yes, then you can do so. Examples of an emergency include: not having any adults to work that shift, or there being more work than usual, such as a private party renting your restaurant's function room or a holiday sale in your store.

Here are some more examples to help you get a feel of what is acceptable and what isn't.

Earl works Saturdays in a clothing store. He usually works out front, replacing clothes on the racks and serving customers, but his contract also lists stockroom duties like taking inventory and unpacking new deliveries. He isn't supposed to work on Sundays, but his boss grabs him at the end of his shift and asks if he can work the next day because they have a big delivery of new stock arriving and two of his usual staff members can't work. It's only a four-hour shift and Earl would be working exclusively on unloading the delivery. As this is an exceptional case where there is more work than usual, it's okay for Earl to be asked, and he accepts.

Angie is a waiter at a well-known restaurant chain. She works two evenings after school from 5 p.m. until 11 p.m. and sometimes takes a Saturday shift if she isn't needed to play soccer on Sunday. She turns up for work on Monday and is asked if she can stay until 2 a.m. because a group has booked a birthday party. Angie refuses because she would be too tired for school the next day. Her manager tries to pressure Angie into working, but she points out that it's in her contract that she doesn't work after midnight on a school night, so her manager backs down.

Iris-Helen works on the weekend in her local cafe. Her duties include clearing the tables, cleaning the dining area, and washing the dishes. She has only been working for a few weeks and hasn't been trained to work the register yet. During the lunchtime rush on Saturday, the cook burns her hand and has to leave. Iris-Helen's manager starts to panic and asks her to take over the cooking, knowing that she doesn't know how to ring up the sales. Iris-Helen doesn't know what to say because she isn't trained to do that either but she doesn't want to let her boss down, so she agrees.

What would you have done in each of these situations? Earl is the only one who really has both options available to him—he can say no if he wants to, but his boss is doing nothing wrong by asking him. Angie shouldn't have been asked to work so late on a school night so she was right to challenge her manager. Iris-Helen was put in a difficult—and dangerous—situation where she was asked to do something she wasn't qualified for. Even though she agreed, her manager should not have asked her, and if she was also injured while working, the manager would have been in big trouble.

If you're ever asked to do something at work that you're not comfortable with, you should always question it. It's better to be too cautious than to put yourself in a dangerous situation.

When You're Not the Problem

Hopefully having a job is a positive experience for you, where you learn new skills and meet people who broaden your views on life. However, there are some bosses, supervisors, and co-workers who you will not gel with, who won't be good at their jobs, and who will take advantage of you. Think of them like the high school bullies of the workplace. If you are treated badly at work there are usually people you can report the behavior to so that things can improve. The one exception is if you are working for a small business where the owner is the person who is treating you badly. I'm afraid, in that situation, you are probably better off looking for another job where you will be better valued.

Workplace incidents that need reporting usually come under one of two categories: bullying and discrimination or sexual harassment. Workplace bullying can look similar to teenage bullying and include name-calling, spreading of rumors, and being unfairly treated; for example, always being given unfavorable jobs that are supposed to be shared, like cleaning the bathrooms. Discrimination at work means you are treated differently from your other co-workers. You might not be given a locker or access to some of the facilities the other staff at the same level of employment use. You might be denied further training or promotion opportunities, have your work judged against higher standards than others, or be more severely punished for mistakes.

Sexual harassment at work can be verbal or physical and it doesn't have to be intentional. Making jokes or asking questions about someone's sex life, orientation, or gender is an absolute no-no at work and should be reported. Comments on someone's outfit, body, attractiveness, or touching them in a way that makes them uncomfortable should also be reported. Your employee handbook will tell you the procedure for making complaints, but it usually involves writing or talking to the person ranked above the person you are complaining about. So if it's another team member whose behavior needs to be kept in check, ask to speak to your shift supervisor or the team manager. If your manager is the problem, you'll need to write to the area manager for the company or the business owner.

Negotiating a Better Deal

Most jobs allow for progress. For example, you could start washing dishes but be promoted to do some cooking, or start as a cleaner but then advance to team leader. Sometimes these positions will be advertised within the company and you can apply for them like any other job. Other times, your boss will approach you about increasing your responsibilities, or you can ask to speak to them if you think you are ready for a step up.

If you're asking for more pay or more responsibility, be prepared to back up your request with examples and proof that you're worthy of the task. If your boss declines, don't argue; instead, ask what you would need to do in order to improve so that you can be considered next time. It can be scary asking for something like this, and there are a lot of adults out there who still feel uncomfortable doing it, but the worst that can happen is nothing changes, and you might be surprised how many times a boss will agree that you deserve a little extra.

Performance Reviews

After a year in your job, you should have a performance review with your manager. They will invite you for a meeting where they will look at how well you've been doing at your job, how committed you've been, and what new skills you've learned. You will both work together to create some targets for the next year. These could include you undertaking some training or getting more experience in a specific area, like sales or customer ser-

KEV CHILTON

vice. It's also a chance for you to let your manager know if there's anything you're unhappy about or anything you would like to aim for.

Chapter Five

Getting That Work/Life Balance

Never get so busy making a living that you forget to make a life. –Dolly Parton

When you're younger, your time is split into two categories: schoolwork and free time. Schoolwork doesn't just take up time at school; it eats up an increasing amount of your free time with homework assignments and projects. Losing this free time can be hard, so when a job comes along and takes even more of your free time, you might feel like there's no time left for the things you enjoy. What it really means is you need to become better at planning and scheduling, so that you can make sure you always have time to do the things that are really important to you.

KEV CHILTON

Perform a Time Audit

There are some things in your daily routine that you can't do anything about. You'll always have school (on a weekday anyway) between certain hours, and you need to make sure you're eating dinner and getting to bed at a reasonable hour. That still leaves you with roughly three to six hours in the evening that you can spend as you wish. Some days, all you'll want to do in that time is binge on Netflix and eat junk food, but that might mean that you'll have to spend the next evening studying for an exam or rushing for a deadline. Better planning would look like splitting two activities over multiple evenings so that you have enough time to do a good job on your schoolwork and still manage to enjoy yourself afterward.

There are lots of different time management strategies out there that promise to be the best way to plan your life. I'm going to share with you the one that's always worked for me. I think it's one of the most straightforward and easy to understand.

Get yourself a piece of paper and split it into three columns labeled "have to," "want to," and "like to." You're going to think about all the things you have to do over the next week—things that take up time in that important slot between finishing school and going to bed—and write them in the first column. This column is for the absolute essentials like band practice, your French tutor, homework assignments, and doctor's appointments.

The next column is for things that you want to do but aren't essential, like extra credit work, attending an online study session, driving lessons, and volunteering. This is probably the hardest column to fill out because lots of things might seem like they actually fit into the first column instead. The trick to working out the difference is to ask yourself if something bad will happen if you don't do something. Not handing in homework will affect your grades and might land you a detention, but skipping a week's driving lesson won't hurt if you have more important things to do.

The final column is for things you enjoy doing, like watching the next episode of a TV show, going skating with your friends, watching your boyfriend's game, or working on a craft project. This column might also include things like exercising, or you might feel like putting that in the "want to" or "have to" columns, especially if you know that skipping your daily yoga practice is going to affect your mental health.

Next, go back to the first column. Add any deadlines or specific days when things have to happen. Then have a look at each activity and decide how long it's going to take you. Some things are easy, like you know that the rehearsal for the school play will take an hour, but try and be realistic when setting times for studying or assignments. If you know that your last English essay took you four hours to write, plan for this one to take five, just in case. It's also good practice to add travel times for activities that happen away from home, because that's going to affect your scheduling too. When you're done with the first column, repeat the process for the remaining two.

Setting Priorities Like an Adult

Now it's time to start slotting activities into your week. Only you know how much free time you have in the evenings and on weekends, so your schedule is going to be personal to you. Start by slotting in everything from the first column. You're not allowed to miss anything out or squeeze anything in by shortening its time, even if that means you don't have a lot of time left for other things. Then fill in the gaps with activities from the other two columns.

Some of your activities have to happen at a certain time, so it's a good idea to put these in first. After all, no one is going to move an after-school club just because you'd rather be finishing your chemistry homework. There are other tasks you'll have that need doing on one day, but you can be flexible with the time. For example, the dog probably isn't going to explode if you walk it an hour later, and you can enjoy an evening run just as much if you do it at 5 p.m. or 9 p.m.

In an ideal world, you would have something from each column on each day so you're spreading out the things that you enjoy in between the work you have to complete. This balance is important for regulating your mood and giving you a sense of achievement, while avoiding panic and anxiety when you realize you've forgotten an important essay or not left yourself enough time to practice for the recital.

Some weeks you'll have lots of time for things from the "like to" column, and other weeks, you'll hardly be able to fit any in. It can be really depressing to realize you can't find time to join your friends at the movies, but it's a much more mature approach to take than pulling an all-nighter to make up for it.

One thing that creating a plan like this can help you with is deciding if you have time for a part-time job and what hours you'll be able to work. If you already have a job, make sure your regular hours go in the "have to" column. Before agreeing to extra shifts, always consult your weekly plan to make sure you can reschedule everything from the "have to" column.

Let's have a look at Tilly's weekly plan and how she organized her time. All the activities in bold are from her "have to" column.

KEV CHILTON

	Monday	Tuesday	Wednesday	Thursday	Friday
8 a.m. - 9 a.m.	Yoga	Go for a run	Yoga	Go for a run	Yoga
9 a.m. - 4 p.m.	School (incl. travel time)	School (incl. travel time)	School (incl. travel time)	School (incl. travel time)	School (incl. travel time)
4 p.m. - 5 p.m.	Swimming lesson	Go to the mall with Stacy		Take CJ to the skate park	Grocery shopping on the way home
5 p.m. - 6 p.m.	Chores (Walk Bruno, clean bedroom)	Go to the mall with Stacy	Study for Geography test (Friday)	Driving lesson	
6 p.m. - 7 p.m.	Biology homework (due Thursday)	Go to the mall with Stacy	Study for Geography test (Friday)	Dance practice	My turn to cook dinner
7 p.m. - 8 p.m.	Biology homework (due Thursday)	Dinner at Five Guys	Chores (Walk Bruno, wash laundry)	Dance practice	English essay (due Monday)
8 p.m. - 9 p.m.	Practice guitar		Netflix time	Chores (Walk Bruno, clean kitchen)	English essay (due Monday)
9 p.m. - 10 p.m.			Netflix time		English essay (due Monday)

Tilly has planned her schoolwork so that she isn't doing it the night before it has to be handed in. She's also tried to leave herself some time before bed in case the work takes longer than she expected, or she can use this as free time to enjoy a hobby or do something relaxing. She has some chores to do but can fit them in around the rest of her activities on that day. On the weekend, Tilly works full day shifts as a waitress, so she doesn't like leaving her homework until then as she's often too tired to concentrate properly.

Organizing Your Free Time

You might have noticed now that your schedule has more things in it that you have to do than things that you like to do. I'm afraid this is part of the transition into being an adult—you have more responsibilities and commitments to others and this means you need to prioritize them over having fun and enjoying yourself. But don't think for one minute that that doesn't mean your own needs aren't important anymore; in fact, they're probably more important than ever because if you aren't well-rested, relaxed, and focused, you won't be working well at your job or your studies. So, while you might not get as much free time as you had when you were younger, you should still be making time for yourself every day.

One way to adapt to this change is to look at slightly different ways to enjoy your favorite activities that might save you some time. For example, do you travel to the gym to go to a class like yoga or spinning? There are hundreds of exercise classes that you can now do online, either by watching a pre-recorded video or attending a live session. If you have the space and the equipment to do this at home instead, you can save yourself the travel time there and back. Video chatting with your friends is also a good way of cutting down travel time, as you don't have to all be in the same place to catch up. There have been lots of developments in technology recently that allows people to enjoy things together from different places, like being able to watch a movie together by syncing the start time and adding an online chat function.

If you really can't find a way to cut down on time spent traveling or waiting around, why not double up by taking an activity with you? Download some TV, a podcast, or an audiobook to your phone to listen to on the bus, or take a book or your study notes with you. It's not quite as relaxing as lying on your bed and reading, but it might be a better use of your time than just staring into space for half an hour. The point is, if there are things you really want to do in your week, outside of school and work, you might need to start finding innovative new ways to fit them in.

Take a Break

Some of us naturally find it easy to organize life, whereas others struggle. Time management is a skill to be practiced and learned, like playing the piano or baking brownies. People who struggle to organize their time well tend to show the following behaviors:

- persistently late for things

- missing deadlines
- can't prioritize multiple projects so they end up doing none of them
- inability to work on more than one thing at a time
- underestimating how long it will take to do something

Always running late can leave you feeling anxious and stressed. You also won't feel like you deserve time to rest and unwind because you still have a lot of things to do, but making time to do something other than work is vital for good mental health. I cover this in more detail in my book *Teens' Guide to Mental Health*, but exercising, meditating, or doing something creative for at least half an hour a day has a wonderfully beneficial effect on your mood, lowers your stress levels, and improves your sleep. Don't underestimate how important it is to spend some time every day on what you need and take a break from school and work.

Chapter Six

Ready to Go Full-Time?

Choose a job you love, and you will never have to work a day in your life. –Confucius

Thinking about your first full-time job might be a few years away yet, but it can be good to have some idea of what to expect when you get there. Schools seem to expect teens to know what they want to do as an adult, when the reality is that plenty of adults haven't got a clue themselves! When I was 16, I wanted to play sports for a living, and while I did play a lot for the police cadets and during my time at the academy, there was no way it was ever going to be my full-time job.

If you ask the adults in your life what their dream career would be, how many do you think would name the one they're currently in? I'd bet you it's not that many, and it goes back to my question in chapter one about why you want a job. Some adults find their careers rewarding and fulfilling, but others just see them as a way to make enough money to do the things they really enjoy.

After finishing school, some of you will go on to further study and others will be looking at going straight into the workplace. Unless you are striking out on your own or joining the family business, you'll have to apply for a full-time job with a resume or application form, just like you would for a part-time job. It's a good idea to keep updating your resume because you'll want to add previous job experience and your college degree (or the fact that you're currently studying) if you have one.

Full-time jobs often have more requirements that you have to meet in terms of experience and qualifications because employers rely more on full-time employees to deliver for the company. Use the information from chapter two to translate your part-time experience into valuable soft skills for your full-time application, because even if you're applying for something completely different, those times spent wiping down tables or refunding ripped clothing will have taught you a lot of useful things.

Is Full-Time Different From Part-Time?

Yes, and not just because you're going to be working more hours. There are some fundamental differences in the types of jobs available and the expectations from your manager, as well as how you might feel at the end of the week. Full-time work is usually defined as working one job for at least 35 hours a week, but you could work the same number of hours across multiple part-time jobs and still notice some differences in the way each job works.

People who work full-time tend to have more responsibilities than those who work part-time. This is because they are at work for all or most of the hours the business operates, so they can offer more continuity of service to their customers. This doesn't matter so much in the retail or food industries, but if you have regular clients to look after, the most important ones are probably going to be given to the people who can work for them every day.

Full-time jobs might offer more job security than part-time jobs because employers have to give you the same number of hours each week. Part-time workers might be on a contract that lets their hours vary, so at busy times they will work more shifts, and in quiet times, they might not be needed. This can make it difficult to plan your finances for the month or schedule your days. However, this flexibility is great if you don't need to work full-time and can use the extra time off to travel and be spontaneous. Sometimes being able to choose to work less when you have other things going on in your life is hugely beneficial.

TEENS' GUIDE TO FINANCIAL INDEPENDENCE

The mental load of working five days in a row can be quite heavy. Eight hours is a long time to be performing at a high level, both mentally and physically. You might find that you don't have the energy to do a lot in the evening, especially when you first start your job. This can be quite depressing, and you might worry that you'll never be able to fit in all the things you want to do in a week, but I can promise you, it does get better as you get more used to the amount of work. It's a bit like training at the gym—when you start, you can't lift the big weights, but after a few weeks, you'll find they're not as heavy as you thought.

Another difference between full-time and part-time work—especially if this is your first full-time job—is that many people feel anxious or undeserving of the job. This is known as impostor syndrome and it's really common. Even legal adults feel this way, but that doesn't mean they aren't capable, and many people worry that their boss will suddenly realize they haven't got a clue how to adult properly. If this sounds like something you feel, try and remember that no one starts their job knowing everything and it's fine to worry about making mistakes when you're still learning. After a while, you will realize you have learned a lot about your job and that you definitely deserve to be there.

Not every type of job is suitable for a part-time role, so you will find there are probably limited choices about the kind of job you would like, if a part-time job is something you're interested in. However, some professions like teaching, nursing, and childcare offer flexible positions for the right people, and it's not uncommon to find a full-time role in these industries that is shared between two people.

Added Benefits

As well as more hours, more money, and greater job security, full-time roles should come with more employee benefits. For one thing, full-time workers are most often paid a salary rather than wages. What is the difference? Wages are paid based on the hours you work, whereas a salary is given as a yearly figure and doesn't change. So, if you have to finish half an hour early one day, or work an extra three hours to hit a deadline, your paycheck won't be any different from normal. Having a salary means you're usually also entitled to sick pay—where you will still be paid even if you haven't been able to go to work because of an illness—and if you're supposed to be working during a national holiday, you'll get that day off and still be paid for it too.

Both full-time and part-time workers are entitled to take paid vacation days, but part-time workers will get a reduced amount based on how many hours they work. Taking paid vacation gives you a chance to still take part in activities you enjoy and it means you don't have to miss events that might happen while you're working, like a special birthday celebration, wedding, or funeral.

Full-time workers may also be entitled to other benefits from their employers, including:

- health care
- stocks and shares
- pension plan
- paid family leave when you have or adopt a child
- gym membership
- travel allowance
- company vehicle
- a payment to your family if you are injured or die while at work

What if I Work for Myself?

The job market is really competitive and there are hundreds of people applying for each job. This has made it more appealing for people to find ways to work for themselves. There are a few different ways to identify as self-employed, and which one you choose will depend on the kind of work you want to do.

- Freelance. You have no fixed company that you work for and are able to offer your services to lots of different places at once. It's up to you to do a good job, and if you do, then business may continue to send you work. Good jobs for freelancing include copywriting, programming, and substitute teaching.

- Contractors hired by a company for a fixed period have to stick to the terms of the contract they offer you. You're in control of what jobs you take, but once you're hired you can only work on that project until it's done. Sometimes your contract will be with your customer, and other times, you can be hired by a firm. For example, if you work in construction, a building company will hire contractors as and when they're needed rather than keeping them on the payroll even when there isn't work to do. Good jobs for contractors include plastering, landscaping, and programming.

- Temp. You can join an agency that specializes in temporary workers, and they'll send you out to work for businesses when they have a short-term gap that needs filling. You can get loads of experience in a number of different fields this way, which is great if you're not sure what to do for a permanent job. You'll have a certain amount of choice of the work you can accept, but you can't ask for specific jobs. Temp workers can work all over the construction industry, office work, and education.

- Small business owner. You own and run the business, are responsible for finding your own paying jobs, and can set your own hours, pay rates, and contract terms. This is what most people think of when they picture self-employment, but it's the hardest to be successful at. Lots of business owners start off as contractors, freelancers, and temps to get experience and build contacts. Sometimes your business will be just you; other times you will hire employees and be responsible for their well-being too. Successful small businesses often include auto repair, local stores, upcycling furniture, and selling crafts online. You could also run your own cleaning, dog-walking, childminding, or taxi service.

Where Do I Go From Here?

It's unlikely that you'll want to stay in exactly the same job for fifty years, so at some point, you'll want to think about career progression and where you would like to see yourself in five, ten, twenty years, or more.

Some jobs seem to have a definite progression in terms of the roles you can move through as you earn promotions. Teaching is a great example, as you go from classroom teacher to head of a subject, head of a year group, deputy headteacher, and then headteacher. However, there are also opportunities to branch out sideways, like becoming a home tutor, working for a company producing educational resources, or moving into politics and influencing how the education system runs. Basically, you can turn your experience and passion for your work into any career progression you can imagine.

So, how do you plan for career progression? Firstly, identify which aspects of your job you are most excited by. Is it the customer interaction, the satisfaction of producing something high quality, or the fact that you get to influence company processes? You can talk to your manager or use the internet to find out some of the extra responsibilities and changes that come with taking a step up. Would this increase your time doing the things you love, or reduce them? Teachers often find that career progression means less time spent in the classroom with the children, and a promotion to foreman at a building site means you spend less time building and more time instructing and managing others. If this step takes you away from the part of your job you are most passionate

TEENS' GUIDE TO FINANCIAL INDEPENDENCE

about, you might need to be a bit more creative. Why not look at other jobs that would give you more chances to work in the way that you want and progress your career by moving to a different field?

If you're looking to stay within the same company, speak to your manager at your annual review and let them know you would eventually like to be considered for a promotion. Ask them what skills you need to demonstrate and if there are any training courses they recommend. There's no reason why you can't start taking little extra steps—look at that, you're demonstrating initiative!—so that when an opening appears, you can show you're ready to step into it.

It's All About the Money

Chapter Seven

Investing, Saving, and All the Hidden Fees

DON'T SAVE WHAT MONEY is left after spending. Rather, only spend the money that remains after saving funds.
–Warren Buffett

Now that you have a job, are you rolling in money? Probably not, but it's nice to have a little extra around to help pay for bills, school supplies, cinema tickets, or to save toward, something in the future. In the olden days, people would keep their money under the mattress or in a jar on the shelf, but that's all a bit impractical nowadays. It's much better to keep it in your wallet, or best still, in a bank account.

You might already have a bank account where your caregivers have been stashing birthday money from distant relatives since you were born. If not, or you want to open a different type of account, you can get your own account by going into a branch and filling out some forms, or filling in those same forms online. Before you go giving your money to just anyone, it's worth thinking about what you want from your bank account and what you need it for, because there are dozens of different products out there and they aren't all the same.

Which Account is Right for You?

You might think you just want an account to keep your money safe, but it's a bit more complicated than that. Do you want to be able to get the money out again, and how often? Is it going to be an account you can spend from using a debit card, or will you need to withdraw money in cash? Are you saving money for a goal, like buying a car or going to college, and would you like your bank to pay interest to help you toward that? Do you even know what interest it? See? Not that simple.

Things will work slightly differently, and be called different names, depending on where you live, but here are the basic kinds of bank accounts you should be able to open as a teenager or young adult. You aren't limited to one account, so you can have a couple of different types or lots of the same type, as long as you use them properly. Always check the requirements for each account carefully to make sure you're eligible, as some aren't suitable for teens and others might need an adult to be named on the account with you.

Checking or Current Account

This is the basic account you're probably thinking of. It can be based at a branch or solely accessible online and, depending on your age, will probably come with a debit card so you can spend the money directly from your account or a bank book or cash card so you can withdraw money from the bank or an ATM. You can also set up direct payments from this account so that bills like your phone get paid automatically every month.

Some checking/current accounts come with added benefits like phone or travel insurance, but you'll often have to pay a monthly fee for these. It's not worth it if you don't need them, so think carefully. Other accounts need you to have a minimum amount that you pay in each month, so make sure you can meet this or choose an account that doesn't have the requirement. If you don't have enough money in your account when you try to make a payment, you can be charged a small fee.

This type of account is perfect for anyone who wants it to act like a giant wallet. You can easily withdraw money or pay for things from your account. If you get paid in cash, like from a babysitting or gardening job, you should open an account that has a physical bank where you can deposit the cash.

Savings Account

Another basic type of bank account. This one isn't meant to be used for everyday spending; rather, it's the equivalent of keeping your money in that savings jar. Savings accounts often have limits on the number of times you can withdraw money, which makes sense, as you're supposed to be saving it, not spending it. They also don't come with a debit card and you can't set up automatic payments from your account.

Savings accounts will pay you interest on the money that you put in there. Interest means you'll get a small payment as a thank you from the bank for leaving your money with them. The amount you'll earn is not a fixed amount but a percentage of the amount you save, and it's given as a yearly amount known as the annual percentage rate (APR). Although it's an annual payout, the interest is calculated daily, so don't think you can make a huge deposit the day before your interest is worked out and get a big reward. It doesn't work like that! Different accounts pay different rates, so it's worth shopping around for the best you can get.

These accounts are for people who want to put their money away rather than spend it now. You can have a specific goal in mind or just want to keep it somewhere safe where it earns a little bit extra, but if you have leftover money each month that you're not using for Starbucks or gas money, it's worth looking at a savings account.

Mixed Account

This goes by a lot of different names, but it's essentially a blend between the two previous accounts. Typically, this is an account that lets you have a debit card and set up payments and still offers a small amount of interest on savings, but it probably limits your monthly withdrawals. Because of this, you'll probably have to deposit quite a high minimum amount each month or have to deposit a lump sum to open it.

This account will probably appeal more once you have a full-time job with good regular earnings. As your paycheck goes into the account and most of the money sits there until it's spent on rent, groceries, and those new jeans you just had to have, it's worth earning a little bit of interest on it. As long as you can make the minimum monthly payments and you always have enough to make any arranged payments, this is a good option for when you're older.

Long-Term Savings Account

These savings accounts come with a higher APR but at the expense of being able to make withdrawals. You can choose the amount of time your money is going to be locked away, but if you withdraw it before that time is up, you won't get any interest payment. There are lots of different lengths you can choose from—from a month to ten years—so it's not like your money will be held hostage forever. If you're saving for a specific goal and know you're not going to need the money until then, this is the best way to get the most out of it, as your APR can be double the size of a normal savings account.

Choosing a long-term savings account is perfect for anyone saving for college, a vacation, a birthday, a car, or a rental deposit. Not being able to withdraw your money means you're not going to dip into it on a whim, but make sure you have other savings or an account that you use if there's ever an emergency.

How Your Money Makes Money

Let's take a closer look at exactly how interest works and how the different types of savings accounts can benefit you. Firstly, let's look at the different types of interest offered—compound and simple. Simple interest pays interest on your initial deposit only, so if you open your account with $100 and it earns 5% APR, you will end the year with an extra $5, regardless of whether you deposit anything else. Compound interest pays interest on everything in your account. So, if you opened the same account with $100 and then paid in $10 each month for a year, you would have an extra $7.90 at the end of the year, plus an extra $120 that you'd saved yourself.

Some savings accounts pay their interest on a yearly basis and others add it to your funds every month. It should all be set out in their terms so you can find this out before opening the account. What's the difference? Probably very little in real terms, but every penny counts when you're trying to raise that total.

Here's how the arithmetic works out:

If your compound interest of 5% is paid monthly over a year, your initial deposit of $100 will become $105.12.

If your compound interest of 5% is paid yearly, your initial deposit of $100 will become $105.

See, pennies. However, if your deposit is larger, say $1,000 or $10,000, the difference is suddenly much more meaningful. So, if you have a larger amount to stash away, always look for monthly interest instead of yearly at the same APR.

Topping Up Your Savings

Some savings accounts give you the best benefits when you deposit a large amount at the start and leave it be, but others are better for regular savers who can put aside the same amount each month. These regular saving accounts often have some of the highest interest rates because you don't have a lot of money in there for the first few months, so they don't have to pay you that much interest. They'll also put a limit on the amount you can save each month, usually only a couple of hundred dollars. If you plan to save the same amount from your wages every month, and you don't have a large initial deposit, this is how you get the best return on your savings (this means you get the most money for nothing!).

After a year, the interest on these accounts usually drops—for example, from eight to two percent—because you now have much more in the account—probably a couple of thousand if you've made the maximum deposit each month. If you still don't need this money—if it's for college, future rent, or even a house deposit—then you can now put it in a long-term savings account and earn even more interest!

Locking Your Money Away

The longer you can go without touching your money, the better your APR will be. Most long-term saving accounts won't pay you any interest if you withdraw before the term is up. For example, you save $3,000 in an account that pays 7.5% APR after three years. At the end of the three-year term, you can withdraw your deposit plus interest, a total of $3,754.34, but if you withdraw it early, you'll just get the $3,000 back. You can't withdraw some of it and leave the rest there.

If you would split your money between something long-term and savings you can access, you can deposit it in two different accounts instead. If you put $2,000 into that long-term account, you'll have $2,502.89 after three years; that's still an extra $500 or so in interest. Put the remaining $1,000 in an instant-access savings account paying a lower rate, and you won't face a penalty if you need to dip into it for bills, repairs, or unmissable concert tickets.

Investing

Earning interest isn't the only way you can earn a little extra from the money you aren't spending. If you definitely aren't going to want it back any time soon and you don't mind a little bit of risk, you could invest your money in something like a business, stocks, property, or artwork. In its simplest form, investing means that you buy something that you intend to sell again and make a profit. However, sometimes this doesn't work out and you could end up getting less money back than you paid in the first place. Why do people invest if there's a risk of losing money? Because, while profits aren't guaranteed, you have the potential to make a lot more money than by just leaving it in an account earning interest.

One of the easiest ways to start investing is in the stock market. You can buy a stock or a share—a small part of a company—and your money gets used by that company, a bit like lending your friend a bit of spare cash so they can buy lunch. In return for your investment, your stocks will usually pay you a small amount every few months. This is called a dividend, and it's the company's way of sharing its profits with the people who bought its stocks, often called shareholders.

You can sell your stocks at any time for their value at the time. So, if your stocks have gone up and are now worth more, you will get a profit, but if they have gone down, you'll lose money. What makes the stocks change value? To put it really simply, it's linked to what the company is doing and how well it's valued in the current economy. Here are a few oversimplified examples so that you get the idea:

You buy a stock in Apple for $5. A few months later, they launch a new iPhone and everyone loves it. Apple stocks go up in value because the company is making lots of money. You sell your stock for $7 and make a profit of $2.

You buy a stock in Mastercard for $10. Things are going well for a bit, but then the economy dips, and people don't want to use their credit cards anymore because they can't afford to pay them back. The value of Mastercard's stocks goes down because they aren't as useful as they used to be. Your stock is now worth $6, so if you sell it you will have lost $4, or you can hang on and hope the value goes up again in the future.

If you're interested in investing you should definitely read up about it in more detail. There are internet guides, YouTube videos, and books available that can teach you how best to manage your money. If you like the idea of higher returns but don't think you want to get involved in managing things that closely, you can take out an investment account where the bank will invest the money for you. They won't take big risks, but because they know the market well, they'll probably still get you a decent profit.

The Many Ways to Pay for Things

I've talked a lot so far about saving money, but I'm betting part of the reason why you wanted to get a job is so you could spend it! Financial freedom means different things to different people—not having to ask caregivers to buy things for you, being able to get the meal you really want rather than the cheapest option, being able to buy someone a gift for their birthday—and having a job makes all of this possible. There's no reason why you shouldn't spend the money you make and use it to enjoy yourself or treat the people you love, but it's a good idea to try and save a little of it as you go, because you never know what will happen in the future.

If you've not had your own bank account before, then it's likely that you've only paid for things with cash (or a card or thumbprint if your school has invested in some swanky technology). Cash is great at helping you budget because once you run out, you can't spend any more, no matter how much you want to. But now that you have an account for your hard-earned wages, you'll probably have a cash card or a debit card that you can use to access your funds.

Cash cards are just for withdrawing cash from the branch or an ATM. Debit cards can be used in stores or online to pay for things by taking the money directly from your bank account and transferring it to the store. You will be asked to insert your card into the reader and type in a special PIN made up of four digits. You'll be given one at random, but you can change it to something easier to remember if you want to. Don't be tempted to set it as anything obvious like your birthday, because if someone steals your card and has some of your personal information, they might be able to guess your PIN and then they can spend your money. Another way to pay is through contactless payments. Contactless payments are a really easy way to pay small amounts, as they don't ask for your PIN so the transactions are much quicker. Some buses and trains use contactless payments instead of tickets so you can just tap your card on the reader to get on and off.

Once you have a debit card, you can activate the mobile payments service on your smartphone if you want to. This means that your phone will save a digital copy of your debit card and you can tap your phone to pay contactless for things instead. Handy if, like me, you often forget to take your wallet with you.

A Warning About Credit Cards

You won't be able to apply for a credit card until you're over 18, but these work completely differently than debit cards. Rather than spending money from your account, a credit card company will pay for things on your behalf and then send you a bill at the end of the month. You can pay this bill in full if you have enough money, or make any amount of part payment over the given minimum, which is usually around 5% of the balance. It means you don't have to have the money in your account to be able to buy something, but beware of just spending the minimum every month, as you will be charged interest on anything you don't pay off, and this is often at a rate of around 30% APR, which is pretty steep.

Credit cards can work well in an emergency. For example, if your car needs repairs immediately and you haven't got enough saved up. You should make a plan to pay the bill as soon as you can so it doesn't end up costing you a lot more in interest. Let me show you a scary example:

You make a payment of $500 on your credit card (30% APR) to cover car repairs on May 15th. On June 1st, you're sent a bill with a minimum payment of $25 that's due by June 30th.

If you pay the full $500, your next bill will be $0.

If you make the minimum payment of $25, your next bill will be $487 (that's $12 interest added, almost half what you already paid off). If you keep paying $25 a month, it will take you two years and three months to pay off the balance and you will have paid an extra $167 in interest.

If you pay $100 a month, it will take you six months to pay off the balance and you will have only paid $36 in interest.

How Banks Make a Profit

Banks are businesses, and like other businesses, they want to make a profit. If you have a basic bank account, you aren't paying anything to use it, but there are still ways in which they can charge you. One of the most common ways is for them to charge you interest on any credit you use. Getting a credit card isn't the only way you can spend money you don't have; lots of bank accounts offer you the chance to have something called an overdraft. This is an amount of money that you can borrow if you need to, usually a couple of hundred dollars, and it acts as a bit of a safety net. If you have a bill coming out on the 15th and your paycheck doesn't clear until the 17th, you can use your overdraft to cover the cost. If you do, it will show up on your account as a negative balance.

How does the bank make money from your overdraft? There are two ways: firstly, by charging you interest, or secondly, by charging a fixed fee. In the first case, every day that you use your overdraft, you will be charged a small amount of interest by the bank, so try not to use it except in emergencies. If your account charges a fixed fee, it will be applied every time you make a payment and there isn't enough money in your account. It will be the same fee whether you use $10 or $100, and lots of accounts have a limit on the number of times you can do this each month—try to go over this limit and you'll incur another fee!

You might be able to tell by now that these fees can quickly add up. Looking at the previous example, if your account allows you to make up to four overdraft payments each month and charges you $30 each time (yes, it can be that much, or even higher), you could end up paying an extra $120 in penalties for not having enough money in your account. Fee charges will always be in your account's terms and conditions, so make sure you know what they are before you sign up. If you think you'll need to use an overdraft facility fairly frequently, do your research and find an account that charges low fees.

Other Credit Options

Saving up for something, earning interest on those savings, and then being able to buy it outright is by far the best way of making large purchases, but I'm a realist and I know that things don't always go to plan. You might be dependent on your car to get to work and school only to have it break down with no hope of repair. If you have to go and replace it but you don't have enough in savings, what do you do? Taking out credit can be a useful option, but you need to do it responsibly.

There are two different types of credit open to you—revolving and installment. Credit cards fall under the first category, as do store cards. The payments are flexible, as long as you pay at least a minimum amount, as is the time you need to pay it back, but you will be charged interest for as long as you are using it. You can borrow more without needing to reapply as long as you don't go over a set limit. Car loans, personal loans, student loans, and mortgages all fall under the second category. Your payments must be a fixed amount every month, which makes them easier to plan for, and you have the credit for a set time. You're charged interest, which is built into the total amount so it doesn't change every month, and you can't borrow more on the same agreement.

When considering credit, you should think about how much you are able to commit to paying back each month. You will be charged interest or late payment fees if you fail to make a payment and these can affect your credit rating (and ability to borrow more money later in life), so you don't want to commit to more than you're reasonably able to pay. With a fixed-term loan, your monthly payments can be lowered by extending the length of the loan, but this will mean you are charged more in interest.

Some people, especially those who have grown up in families with money worries or who have gone through moments of financial hardship, can struggle to manage their money well. If you've always seen your caregivers taking out loans to cover the basics, you might assume that it's normal to always be in debt. While it is sometimes unavoidable, borrowing money all the time is not something that everyone does, and while it might be necessary to take out a loan for essential repairs, you shouldn't be using credit carelessly to buy luxury items and treats all the time.

KEV CHILTON

Chapter Eight

Budgeting 101

A BUDGET IS TELLING your money where to go instead of wondering where it went. –Dave Ramsey

Once you have money in your pocket—or your bank account—it's so easy to spend it. You'll be surprised how quickly it can disappear even if you never buy anything big. A donut here, a movie ticket there... it all adds up. A good way to see where your money is going, and if there's anything you can cut back on, is to keep a diary of your monthly spending. If you spend money using your debit card, your bank will keep a record, but you should also write down anything you spend cash on. At the end of the month, sit down with your records and sort your spending into groups like food, travel, essentials, fun, and savings.

Do you notice that one category has more spending than any other? Are these things that you have to buy like groceries or your phone bill, or are they treats and little extras? Look at the places you're spending money too. If you go to the movies or a sporting event, do you also buy drinks and food? If you go shopping with your friends, do you always end up staying for a meal? These extra, unplanned purchases can more than double the cost of your evening without you realizing it.

If you want to start saving some money, you're going to have to reduce your spending. Plan ahead and take your own snacks when you go out for the evening, or if you know that having to buy a meal is likely, budget for that in the cost of the day and spend less elsewhere instead.

Picking Financial Goals

In chapter one, I asked you to think about the reasons why you wanted to get a job, and now I'm going to ask you to examine why you want to have money. You might think the answer is obvious—to buy things—but, like an onion, that statement has layers. Do you want to buy something now or save for the future? Do you want to buy things for yourself or do you need to help others make payments? Maybe you don't want to buy things at all; instead, you want to create some financial security so you know you'll never have to miss a meal or go without heat or water at home.

TEENS' GUIDE TO FINANCIAL INDEPENDENCE

We've already looked at how different bank accounts can help you do different things with your money, and in order to choose the right one you need to know what your money is for, or at least how much of it you want to spend and how much you want to save.

First things first, do you have a long-term saving goal? If the answer is yes, do you know roughly how much you'll need? If it's for something like a car or a vacation, you probably do; however, if it's for college or a nest egg, the final amount just needs to be as much as you can manage.

If you know how much you need to save and when you need it by, you can work out how much you have to save each month to get there. If that amount is too high for your current financial situation, you'll have to look at either changing your goal or finding some extra work. Here are two examples:

Woody wants to be able to buy a new gaming console, which costs $450. He knows the price isn't going to increase in the future, which makes it easy for him to try and budget. He already has $50 from his birthday saved up, so he needs $400 more. Woody works 8 hours a week at $4.50 an hour; that's $36 he makes from each shift, which is about $144 every month. He decides he can save $50 each month (he needs $70 each month for travel costs and the rest is for *going out with his friends). At this rate, it will take Woody eight months to save up for his gaming console.*

Hattie's uncle has promised to sell her his old car if she can raise the money by her birthday. She needs to save $800 in six months or he'll sell it to someone else because he needs the money. Hattie makes $40 a week babysitting for the neighbors on Tuesday and Friday nights and in six months that will add up to $1,040, but she can't save all of it because she has to pay for the bus and her school lunches. Hattie works out that she will need to save $31 every week ($800 divided by 26 weeks) in order to reach her goal, but at the moment, she can only afford to save $20. She asks her neighbors if they would recommend her to their friends and is offered another regular sitting job for Wednesday night at $25. She can now save $45 a month and will definitely have enough for the car and have some left over to pay toward the insurance.

Saving or Spending?

Even if you don't have a specific goal in mind, it's a good idea to put a little of your money into savings each month so that you can use it in the future. College, renting your own place, traveling, or owning a car might be many years away yet, but the earlier you start saving even just a little bit, the easier it will be to afford when the time does come.

TEENS' GUIDE TO FINANCIAL INDEPENDENCE

Do you remember the time audit you did in chapter four? We're going to do a similar one now, this time focusing on how you're spending your money. You can either track your actual spending like I suggested at the start of this chapter or you can make an educated guess, but the more accurate your budget is, the easier it will be to stick to it.

Draw up three columns and label them "have to buy," "want to buy," and "like to buy." The "have" column is for expenses that come up every month and have to be met; things like your phone bill, subscriptions, bus pass, repayments, and school lunches. By each one, try and give the monthly amount you spend. You should also add annual costs like your car insurance to this column, but divide the amount you spend by twelve to find the monthly figure.

The next column is for things you want to buy that aren't part of your regular spending and could be more expensive than other things you usually buy. This could be birthday presents, replacements for things that are getting old or have stopped working, tickets to a one-off event, or anything else that wouldn't come under normal spending. Again, try and budget for an amount—this should be easy if you have specific things in mind.

In your final column, you're going to list all the things you like buying and that you can afford to do on a regular basis. This is where all those coffees, burgers, hobbies, clothes, and other little treats go; things that you don't need to save for or put much thought into.

Everyone's audit is going to look completely different, so don't worry about whether your spending is normal, extravagant, wasteful, stingy, or bare. If most of your money is taken up by items in the "have" column, you're not going to have a lot of things in the "like" column. If there aren't many things in the "have" column, your spending is going to be more in the "want" and "like" columns. We're going to look at how to make the most out of what you have, whatever that looks like.

The items in your "want" column are going to be the things that you are looking to save money for. Even if there isn't anything in it right now, there will probably be something that comes up in the future, and already having a pot of savings that you can spend is going to be really useful. Deciding on how much money to save and how much to have available for spending can be tough. You need to balance a couple of different factors and make sure you don't run out of money and rack up a load of fees when you can't make payments. Let's go through a couple of budgeting methods that will help put you in control of your money.

Put Your Goals First

TEENS' GUIDE TO FINANCIAL INDEPENDENCE

This approach works best when you have a long-term saving goal in mind. Work out how much you need to save and how long you have to reach your goal. Divide the total by the number of months to work out the minimum you need to save each month to hit your target. For example, if you want to save $150 for a concert ticket that goes on sale in five months, you'll need to save $30 per month. Working out your goals this way will help you see if they're achievable or not.

Once you know how much you need to save, you have to commit to putting that amount aside each month and not spending it. Any money you have leftover can then go toward your spending, and if that isn't enough for everything you want to do, you'll have to change your plans. Using the above example, if you earn $100 a month and save $30, you will have $70 left to spend.

The 50/30/20 Rule

When you have a full-time job and income, this method can help you balance where your money goes, but it's useful to learn it now so that it becomes a good habit. It's great for when you don't have a set saving goal, but you know you don't want to spend all your money at once.

The figures above are the percentage of your wages that should be going toward bills and essentials (50%), everyday and fun spending (30%), and savings (20%). So, if you earned $100 a month, that's $50 you can spend on things like the bus fare, your phone bill, and school lunches. You'll then have $20 to put into your savings account and $30 to treat yourself with. If you have anything spare, you can either roll it over til the following month or add it to your savings.

Take Away Total Rule

This is a slightly more flexible version of the percentage rule that takes into account what your actual bills and goals are. Add up everything that you have to pay for each month and take this away from your monthly earnings. Next, work out how much you need to save each month to reach your goal, and then take this away from what's left. Still got some money in your pocket? This is your spending money.

Here's the arithmetic with a real example: You earn $100 a month and have to pay $32 for your phone bill and $15 for Netflix. 100-32-15=53, so you have $53 left, but you want to save $30 for that concert ticket, so your actual spending money for the month is $23.

Priorities

You might have noticed that there's a clear set order here for how you pay for things, and unfortunately spending on the fun things is right at the bottom. However, if you spend your money without planning ahead, what could happen? Let's find out.

Jamie has just started working at his local fast-food restaurant. He has to pay for his car insurance ($153 per month), and he also wants to save up for a new guitar. He gets $4.25 an hour and works 4 hours on Friday night and 8 hours on Saturday. His first paycheck is $204 and he's really excited. He made plans to meet his friends for a movie ($9.70) and treated himself to a large drink and nachos combo ($15) and ice cream afterward ($4.50). Over the week he buys three coffees ($16.50), a burger ($4), a brownie ($3) and downloads the new Green Day album ($15). When his insurance payment is due he only has $136.30 left in his bank account so he's charged $37 for an overdraft payment.

Had Jamie budgeted better, he would have worked out that he only had $51 to spend that month. He only overspent by $16.70, but it ended up costing him an extra $37 as a bank fee. See how easy it is to spend too much? If Jamie had waited a few more weeks for the album and gone without that brownie, he would have been okay.

Thinking Long-Term

Your budget doesn't have to be set in stone and you should review it regularly. Lots of things will change as you get older, including how much you earn, what you're saving for, and what you have to pay for out of your own pocket. If your expenses go up but your wages don't, you might need to look for extra shifts or consider cutting back on some of your spending. If you start earning more but don't need to spend it, think about putting a higher percentage of your wage into savings so that you can use it later.

Choosing where you have to stop spending money can be hard. Start by looking at your regular monthly spending—the things you have to pay for. Is there anything here that you can change? Maybe you're paying for a music streaming service and could switch to a free plan (and tolerate the frequent advertisements), or you aren't really using your gym membership and it would be cheaper to just pay as you go. What about taking a lunch to school instead of buying one there? Making your own is always going to be cheaper; you can pack all of your favorites, and you won't have to fight anyone for the last slice of pizza.

Even if you're not finding money is tight, why don't you try having a month where you take your own food and drink to school or when you go out? You might be surprised how much extra cash you have at the end of the month. A friend of mine used to get a sub and Starbucks for his lunch every workday—that's about $10 a day, $50 a week, $200 a month—until his girlfriend moved in and made his lunch for him. Okay, so she wasn't packing him fancy meats on Italian bread every day, but it was tasty and made with love, and a whole month of homemade lunches ended up saving them around $150!

Other Ways to Save

If there really isn't any wiggle room in your budget and you don't have any money left over to enjoy yourself, it can feel isolating. You want to go out and spend time with your friends and do all the same things they're doing, but not being able to afford to join them can be upsetting or make you feel embarrassed about not having as much money as they do. Why don't you try talking to your friends and see if you can plan some cheaper activities that involve everyone? Some of them probably feel the same way you do and will be glad someone else mentioned it first.

Here are a few suggestions that you and your friends could do to save money and still have fun:

- Rent a movie instead of seeing it at the cinema. Whoever is hosting pays for the movie (still cheaper than a cinema ticket) and everyone else has to bring one snack or drink to share. Take turns to host and you can set themes to match the film, like sci-fi-themed food or everything must be red!

- Instead of picking up cakes and snacks after school, why not learn to bake your own? Challenge each other by competing to make the best cookies, brownies, or muffins, and then vote for your favorites. Or nominate someone to bake each week and then enjoy Friday treat day—on them.

- Spent too much money over the summer? Welcome to Save-tember! Challenge everyone to save as much as they can for one month only. Maybe everyone chooses one thing to give up—like taking the bus or dessert at lunch—and adds up how much they save by the end of the month. The winner gets bragging rights, but everyone's a winner because you've all saved some cash.

- Instead of going out for dinner, pack a potluck picnic. Design the menu together and then give everyone their own dish to prepare. Have your picnic in the mall, at the movies, or in the park. Or just arrange for everyone to bring their own meals, but get them to bring an extra portion to share so that everyone has enough. It's a great way of trying new things and sharing food from different cultures.

- Download an autosave app that pinches pennies

from your account and sticks them in savings when you aren't looking. One of my favorite functions is that you can "round up" your purchases and pocket the difference—a $2.99 milkshake becomes a $3 purchase, and the one cent gets put in your savings. You could each try out a different one and maybe even write a review for your school paper/newsletter and help other students save too.

- Take it in turns to help each other clear out your closets and get rid of some outfits you don't wear. Pop them on a selling app, hold your own second-hand sale, or swap them among yourselves. If anyone in the group is creative and talented, they could even have a go at embroidering designs on them or cutting them up and resewing them into original statement pieces. What a fun way to get "new" clothes!

Chapter Nine

Grown-Up Expenses

NEVER SPEND YOUR MONEY before you have earned it.
–Thomas Jefferson

At the moment, most of you don't have a lot of bills and outgoings that you need to spend your money on. You can use it for fun things and leave the adults in your life to spend their money on groceries, rent, and new furniture. They might ask you to help out a little bit, especially as you get older and start working more hours; it all depends on your circumstances and what your caregivers think is fair. Some teens make it to adulthood without anyone speaking to them about how to manage their money and others have had firsthand experience of budgeting and bills.

TEENS' GUIDE TO FINANCIAL INDEPENDENCE

Regardless of your situation, it's always a good idea to look ahead to some of the financial responsibilities you'll have as an adult and think about some of the ways you can make sure you have enough money to cope with unexpected problems.

Why Adults Never Have Any Money

Believe me, it isn't because we're out every night splurging on lobster and buying front-row tickets to *Hamilton*. Most adults are good at managing their money, but that doesn't mean they will still have enough to do everything they want. In the previous chapter, I showed you how to decide which of your expenses were absolutely necessary and which were treats if you could afford them, and unfortunately, as you grow up, you get many more things in that first group that takes up a larger percentage of your paycheck.

Some of you might know exactly what your household spends the money on and how much groceries, utilities, and gas cost each month. Others will have absolutely no idea, although you might be able to make an educated guess. To make things completely clear, here's a pretty comprehensive list of things that you'll have to pay for as an adult:

- rent

- local or property taxes
- groceries
- toiletries
- transport (public fares or upkeep of your car)
- utilities (gas, electric, and water)
- broadband
- phone contract
- TV service
- insurance

On top of this, there are other things you'll want to buy, like new clothes, books, birthday presents, or cinema tickets, and occasional payments for repairs, new household goods, or a well-earned vacation. You might find you have enough money to pay for these things without needing to save up, but other times you won't.

I would love to be able to give you an estimate for what each of those items cost, but it varies so much depending on where you live. As a general rule, the first half of the items on that list are more expensive in cities than in rural areas, even in the same part of the country. To give you one example, I once rented a whole 3-bedroom house in a village in the north of England for £600 per month and my friend paid £900 per month for one room in a shared house in the city of London! The second half of the list will be priced differently by different companies, so you can often shop around to find the best deal.

I also can't give you a typical figure that you might expect to earn as your starting salary. There are just too many different factors—what industry you work in, what qualifications you have, where you live (again!). Someone leaving school at 18 with poor grades who starts an unskilled job will earn less than someone leaving university with a top degree and a job in finance. Your starting full-time salary could be anywhere from $10,000 to $100,000, and those may seem like exaggerated figures, but they're not.

Whatever you are earning, you need to make sure that the choice you make about how you spend your money is reasonable. If you earn $10,000 but spend like you earn $30,000, it won't be long before you are in a serious amount of debt.

What's Necessary and What's Fun

When I was younger, my parents decided they would start giving me a small allowance every week that I could spend on things like sweets, toys, and magazines. I was really excited and wrote down all the things I wanted to buy, added up what it would cost, and told them how much they needed to give me. Once they'd finished laughing, they explained that it doesn't work that way. You can't just decide you're going to earn a certain salary, although you can negotiate pay rises with your manager once you've been there a while, so you need to learn to tailor your spending to match your income, even if that means making some compromises.

You might want to live by yourself in a studio apartment, but is it reasonable on your salary? Would you have enough money after your rent is paid each month to pay for the rest of your bills and do the things you want to do? Sharing an apartment with two other people would mean splitting the rent three ways, as well as sharing cost of the utilities and taking turn with the chores. For many young people, this is a worthwhile compromise.

It's a good idea to sit down and think about what a month in your life is going to look like with different types of budgets. Think of it a bit like getting different options for streaming services or memberships; one where it's just the basics, another with upgraded features, and then the luxury full service. For your luxury life, maybe you rent your own place, drive to work, eat dinner out once a week, take a couple of classes at the gym, and spend the weekend going out with your friends. Now try and see how this fits with your actual monthly earnings (or predicted earnings if you're still applying for jobs). Does your monthly wage cover all these options? Does it leave room for you to save some money for the future?

If not, then you need to look at the next budget option, your life with some upgrades, and some basic features. What could you drop without too much trouble? Swapping gym classes for online classes can save you a good chunk of money, not just on membership fees but other incidentals like the latte you pick up on the way home afterward. Instead of eating out once a week, would getting takeout be cheaper? Or how about just going out once a month but making the destination somewhere special?

If you price that up and find you're still struggling on your budget, it's time to look at the basic package. If possible, live at home to save on paying rent, and carpool, walk, or take public transport to work. Workout with free YouTube videos and have your friends over instead of going out. Meal prep in advance so you don't need to worry about cooking every night and you're not tempted to order in when you can't afford it.

A Quick Note About Taxes

Once you start earning money, you need to learn about income tax. This is a percentage of your salary that is given to the government to pay for services that everyone has access to, like well-maintained roads, working traffic lights, public libraries, and the police. All those things you thought you got to enjoy and use for free? Surprise! They're actually paid for by adults.

If you're an employee, you'll notice some money being taken from your paycheck by your employer. This is the easiest way to pay taxes because they'll work out the right amount for you and make sure it's paid on time. In some countries you'll have to also fill out a form once a year so that the government can check you're paying the right amount. If you're self-employed, you'll have to fill out some forms too and you'll need to work out how much to pay yourself. Make sure you factor this in when budgeting what to do with your earnings so you don't spend the money you need to save for your tax bill. Sometimes you end up paying too much or too little. If this happens, you'll be contacted and either sent a rebate—where you get back your money if you sent too much—or asked to pay extra.

The amount of tax you have to pay depends on your yearly salary. Some countries start charging you taxes on everything you earn, whereas others don't ask you to pay anything until you earn over a certain amount—often called the threshold. Anything you earn over the threshold will be taxed at a set percentage. For example, if the threshold is $13,000 and you earn $20,000, then you will pay taxes on the extra $7,000. Some countries have thresholds where the percentage of tax rises. This means that people who earn more money will generally end up paying more in tax. For example, if you earn $20,000, you'll pay 10% on everything you earn up to $13,000, and 12% on the remaining $7,000.

You should find out how the tax system works where you live so that you can be properly informed and don't accidentally get in trouble for not paying them. You'll find this information online or you can speak to your caregivers, other family members, or your manager and ask them to help you work things out. If you're working a full-time job and earning a good salary, you might be able to afford a financial advisor to help you fill out the forms and plan your spending and saving.

Planning Ahead

If this all sounds daunting and scary, you aren't alone. Almost everyone has felt unprepared for dealing with budgets, debt, taxes, and savings at some point in their lives—usually right at the start of adulthood! But also, everyone else has to deal with these things, so they can't be that unmanageable. In fact, you'll probably find that a lot comes naturally once you get there. If you've got some common sense, you'll know that it's not a good idea to spend money you don't have, and thanks to online banking apps, you can even check your account from the store to see if you can afford name-brand groceries or if you should stick to the own-brand ones this week.

KEV CHILTON

If you're on a tight budget, putting anything away in savings can be difficult, not just physically but emotionally. Is it really worth saving a spare $20 this month when you've had to turn down invitations from your friends five times already? Yes, it is. Planning for the future is really important, and I don't mean so you can have a vacation in the summer or afford the latest gaming console; savings are important to have so you can cope in an emergency. If it's so hard to save $20 each month, how hard is it going to be if your washer breaks or your car needs urgent repairs?

Having an emergency fund, no matter how small, can really make a difference. Life is full of surprises and not all of them are good. Unexpected bills, rent raises, unemployment, and illness can hit at any time and make life difficult. Knowing that you have something to fall back on will be a huge relief. Here's a quick guide on what your savings could be worth if you save different monthly amounts:

- If you save $25 a month, after one year, you will roughly have enough to replace or repair pretty much any appliance in your home, replace all four tires on your car, or pay for an emergency plumber or electrician to visit.

- If you save $50 a month, after one year you will roughly have enough to fix most engine problems in your car, purchase a six-month ticket for public transport, or cover a couple of weeks of unpaid sick leave from work.

- If you save 10% of your salary every month, after one year, you will have enough money to last for five weeks if you lose your job.

- If you save 25% of your salary every month, after one year, you will have enough money to last for three months if you lose your job.

I've mentioned a couple of times that it's worth saving money now even if you don't have a specific goal in mind, and that's because you have fewer outgoings and bills now than you ever will have. Saving $50 a month when you don't have rent to pay or groceries to buy is much easier when you know it doesn't mean having to go without something else. By building up your emergency fund early, you'll have access to it sooner if you need it.

Getting your first job after finishing your education could take some time, and if you have no savings to spend while you're looking but all the regular expenses of living independently, you're going to find life very hard. Once you get into debt, whether that's paying with credit cards, borrowing from family, or just avoiding the landlord, it's extremely difficult to get out of it. You will always be playing catch up, unable to save anything for the future because you're using it to clear existing debts. Be smart and save what you can, when you can.

If You Have to Borrow Money, Be Smart

If disaster strikes and you don't have enough in savings to cover what you need, borrowing money can be a useful option. There are a few ways to do this: credit cards and loans.

- Credit cards: These have the highest interest rates, but they are the easiest way to make a purchase on credit, and you can vary your repayments. If you already have a card, you don't need to reapply each time you want to buy something. Use your credit card if you know you have money coming in soon but you just don't have enough yet.

- Loans: These are useful for bigger purchases, like a replacement car, boiler, or essential home repairs. Lower interest rates and fixed monthly payments make it easy to budget. You'll need to have a good credit score and how much you can borrow will depend on your earnings and budget—you'll have to apply each time you want a loan and be assessed each time. You won't be successful if the lender doesn't think you will be able to afford the repayments.

TEENS' GUIDE TO FINANCIAL INDEPENDENCE

Repaying credit over time can be costly because interest will be added on for each month you have borrowed the money for. When looking at repayments, there are some tricks to help your money go further.

- Some credit cards offer interest-free rates if you transfer the balance from another card. All you'll have to pay is a small transfer fee. Once you transfer your money, it won't be earning interest anymore for the duration of the free period, but it will still need paying off before the end of this period or it will start earning interest again.

- If you have a lot of money earning high interest on credit cards, you could speak to the bank about consolidating these debts into one loan. This will dramatically cut your interest rate, often by as much as 70%. However, it will mean you have to commit to regular monthly payments, and you won't be able to miss one.

- If you can't reduce the interest rates on your current debt, make sure you pay the one with the highest interest rate first. Prioritize clearing debt over putting money in a savings account because the interest you earn on your savings will be much less than the interest you're charged on your borrowings.

KEV CHILTON

What to Do if You Don't Have Enough Money

If you can't pay your bills or your rent, don't just ignore them. Lots of lenders are willing to help if you speak to them before you start missing payments. Banks can give people payment holidays where they pause repayments for a few months, but they will only do this if you tell them about your circumstances; for example, losing your job or being ill and unable to work. Utility companies might be able to offer you a cheaper tariff or a repayment plan. Remember, it's in their best interests to help you pay what you owe them.

If you find that you can't afford your rent anymore, you should let your landlord know and start looking for somewhere cheaper to live or consider moving back home to build up your savings again. Most rental agreements have a short notice period, so you'll only have to cover another month or two. However, if you stop paying your rent your landlord will take it out of your security deposit.

Chapter Ten

Financing for University

*Y*OU HAVE TO GO *to college. You have to get your degree. Because that's the one thing people can't take away from you is your education. And it is worth the investment.*
–Michelle Obama

Deciding to continue your education to a higher level can have a lot of benefits. Not only will you have a more in-depth knowledge of your chosen subject, which can lead to a more specialized job and higher salary, but you'll also meet people from different communities who will challenge you and broaden your understanding of the world. Even if you've been lucky enough to visit other places on vacation, you can't truly understand other cultures, communities, and classes until you've lived with them and worked together.

However, to get the best out of your university education, you have to be motivated to work, because no teachers are going to be chasing you for assignments and keeping you behind if you miss one. It might sound obvious, but you also need to be interested in the subject you chose to study, otherwise you're going to find it hard to get motivated. Lots of people go to university to study something because their family wants them to or it's expected of them, but if you'd rather get an art degree than become a doctor or a lawyer, you're not going to be focused enough in class to get a good grade.

University is expensive and most of you will have to borrow a lot of money to be able to afford it. Why waste that money studying something you don't care about and risk coming out with poor grades at the end? If you're on the fence about whether university is for you, you could always take some time out and travel or work for a few years first, there's no hard and fast rule that you have to go when you're 18. In fact, many people go to university later in life once they have a better idea of what they want to study and how it can help them in their chosen career.

Basic Costs

Much like trying to give you a rough figure for rent and utilities, telling you how much university costs is impossible. The best thing you can do is use the internet to research typical costs for the universities that you are interested in. I guarantee you won't be the only one to ever search that up and most universities have typical rates listed somewhere on their website. I'll try my best to give you some ballpark figures.

In the United States:

- The average cost of community college is $2,055 per semester. Out-of-state students can pay double what in-state students pay for tuition and fees.

- The cheapest in-state community college fees are in California, the most expensive are in South Dakota.

- The average cost of attending university for a four-year course is $36,436. This includes tuition, fees, books, and living expenses.

- The average cost of room and board is $12,111 per year.

- Out-of-state students can pay as much as three times the cost of in-state tuition fees.

- The most expensive university is Columbia University in New York City. (Hanson, 2023a & Hanson, 2023b)

KEV CHILTON

In the United Kingdom:

- The average cost of a university degree for UK students in 2023 was £66,560. This includes tuition fees, accommodation, and living costs.

- If you live in Scotland and go to a Scottish university, you won't have to pay any tuition fees. The same goes for Republic of Ireland students studying in their own country.

- University students spend about £1,038 per month. On average, £439 of this goes on rent, £133 on groceries, and £79 on bills.

- London is the most expensive city to study in; so much more expensive, in fact, that you can actually borrow extra financial aid if you choose to study there.

- International students wanting to study in the UK can expect to pay up to £20,000 per year in tuition fees. (Allingham, 2023)

Unless your parents can afford to pay for everything or you earn a full scholarship, you're going to come out of university with a serious amount of debt. Some degrees will help you gain access to a highly-paid career, especially if you go into private medicine, the financial sector, or computer programming. Having a university degree is no longer a guarantee that you'll get a higher starting salary in your first job; however, it can help you progress faster and reach further up the company hierarchy over the course of your career.

Schemes to Help

The reason students accumulate so much debt at university is because they take advantage of financial loans, which are available specifically to cover the cost of tuition, fees, and accommodation. These loans make it possible for people of all incomes and backgrounds to access higher education by giving them the money upfront and delaying repayments until after they have graduated.

In the United States, there are two types of student loans for university: federal and private. Federal student loans have a fixed interest rate and a fixed term for repayment. You can apply through the Federal Student Aid website. Private loans can offer variable interest rates, which are usually higher than the federal loans.

In the United Kingdom, all student finance applications are dealt with by Student Finance through the gov.uk website in England or through separate websites in Scotland, Wales, and Northern Ireland. You can apply for a tuition fee loan to cover, well, tuition fees! There's also a maintenance loan to cover living costs. There's a basic amount that is available to everyone and a top-up that is available to low-income families. There's also an extra top-up if you're studying and living in London. You don't need to start repaying your loan until your yearly salary is over their repayment threshold and the amount you pay each month is linked to your income. Twenty-five years after graduating, anything you haven't paid back will be wiped out, so some people never pay back their student debt.

While student loans have to be repaid, there are other financial aid options available to some students that do not have to be repaid. These come in the form of grants, scholarships, and bursaries.

- Grants are usually means-tested, which means that they go to people whose families don't earn a lot of money. You have to apply for grants and will be asked to prove your income or your family's income. If you or your family receive government benefits, like unemployment or disability allowance, you should be eligible for university grants.

- Scholarships are granted based on your achievements—academic or extracurricular. Sometimes they will pay for your entire tuition, and other times, they will just contribute part of it. These aren't awarded in the same way as other student aid; they are usually paid by a university or a company and you have to apply directly. Some scholarships have restrictions on who can apply, like specifying your race, religion, or location, but most are open to everyone. A university could choose to award you a scholarship if you are one of the top athletes or academic students who apply and you demonstrate that you would have difficulty funding the place without their help.

Working While You Study

Lots of students work part-time around their lectures. In fact, a lot of campuses even provide jobs in student-run coffee shops, bars, food outlets, and stores. The same sort of jobs that appeal to highschoolers also work really well for university students, mostly because they let you organize your shifts around your lectures and you can adjust how often you work—more shifts in the holidays and fewer when you have exams.

Don't forget that most lecturers and professors live either on campus or close by and they might be happy to hire their students for babysitting, house-sitting, or gardening jobs too. There's absolutely no reason why you wouldn't be able to take your self-employed business with you when you head off to university; it'll just take you a little while to get started again.

KEV CHILTON

Going It Alone

Sometimes, even with all these options, the financial aid system just doesn't work in your favor. It assumes a lot of things, like the fact that if your caregivers have the money, they will pay toward your tuition. Some of you will have caregivers who don't want you to go to college, who refuse to put any money toward it, or who try to bribe you to study what they want by only funding that particular course. Some of you will be caregivers yourself, either looking after young children or caring for the medical needs of adults in your life, or you won't feel that you can afford college because you're the sole income earner. It's tough, trying to follow your dreams when you have extra obstacles in the way, but there are options out there for you too.

Your local community college might not be as prestigious as some of the universities your friends are going to, but it is much more accessible and will still allow you to work and live at home if you're needed. Online universities like the Open University offer a flexible way to study for your degree in your own time. In fact, lots of universities offer part-time courses that will take twice as long to complete but let you work two or three days a week.

If you've got your heart set on the traditional campus university experience, why not take a gap year or two to work full-time and fund your own learning? Some jobs will even let you take time off for studying and return to your job later, or allow you to work part-time while you learn. You might even find a company that will pay toward your degree; how amazing would that be?

Chapter Eleven

Don't Get Sucked In

*D*ON'T DWELL ON WHAT *went wrong. Instead, focus on what to do next. Spend your energies on moving forward toward finding the answer.* –Denis Waitley

Your generation is growing up in a world that's far more digitized than the one your parents and caregivers knew when they were young. There are some wonderful benefits to that—access to information, video calling, online shopping—but among all of these are some pretty big downsides. You don't need to pull off a dangerous bank robbery to steal someone's money anymore, just some decent computer skills and a gullible victim. There are criminals out there who make their money by stealing from other people and you need to make sure you're smart with your cash and don't fall for any online scams.

Keeping Yourself Safe

Most people manage their money online now, using mobile apps or online banking websites. It's simple to do and you can see your money at any time of the day or night, move it between accounts, and use it to pay bills. But anyone who gets ahold of your login details can do it just as easily, and before you even know something is up, they could change your password, lock you out of your account, and transfer your money to their own accounts.

Banks understand how important it is that you can trust them with your money, so they invest heavily in secure encryption methods that make it almost impossible for someone to guess your password. So, how do criminals get around this? They find ways to make you give them your password instead! You might think no one would be that stupid, but some of these schemes are very sophisticated, like emailing you pretending to be your bank and asking you to click a link to access your account. The link will take you to a fake login page that looks identical to your bank's page, but when you enter your username and password, the scammers will be able to log into your real account.

Here are the top rules to remember to protect your bank account from scammers:

- Your bank will never email you and ask for your

details; they know it isn't a secure way to do it. Unless you're expecting an email from them—for example to confirm a new account opening—if they need you, they'll mail or call you.

- Don't click on links in emails if you think they could be suspicious. Type your bank's web address into the address bar instead and go there directly. If there's a message from your bank in your account, you'll know the contact is genuinely from them.

- Check what email address your emails are coming from. It might say it's from the bank, but if the address itself is something random, it's definitely a scam.

- You should check your bank account regularly and look through the transactions. If you spot anything you don't remember buying, call your bank immediately and ask them to cancel your cards.

- Use different passwords for all your accounts and don't use any information about yourself that could be easy to guess, like FidoDog2004. Otherwise anyone who knows the name of your first pet can access your email, banking, and social media profiles.

- Use an online wallet like PayPal for online shopping. It stores your bank details in one place and then pays from your PayPal account rather than asking you to enter your bank details into every website you buy from. This is much safer and makes it less likely that your card details will be stolen.

- Shop online at reputable sites. If somewhere seems too good to be true, it probably is. There's no way you can actually get that brand new PS4 for $50; step away now!

Spotting a Scam

Scams work because they rely on people to trust what they're told. Some of the most common ones will also prey on your emotions and make out that you're helping someone in need; others promise you rich rewards if you can just pay some admin fees upfront. So to be extra vigilant, here are some of the top scams to avoid:

- You get a message claiming to be from the new number of a relative, or they're texting you off someone else's phone. They're in trouble and asks if you could please send them a small amount of money for food, bills, or the train home.

- You get an email confirming your purchase of something expensive or claiming you've signed up to a new membership and the payment is about to be taken. There's always a link to click if you want to "change your mind" before you card is charged. Don't click the link!

- You're contacted by the tax office because you haven't paid enough and they threaten to arrest you if you don't make that payment.

- An anonymous email warns you that they have webcam footage of you doing something embarrassing and they'll release it online unless you pay their blackmail fee.

- Congratulations! You've won a huge prize on a lottery that you didn't enter. They'll transfer the money to you right away, but first you have to pay a substantial sum as an admin fee.

- Someone you don't know has died and they chose you to inherit their fortune, but again, there's an upfront admin fee.

- You're contacted by a random stranger who needs a bank account in your country to receive their inheritance or prize winnings. They'll let you keep some of it if you help them out and pay their transfer fees upfront.

It's worth remembering that scammers don't always want a lot of money from you. In fact, they're more likely to succeed in swindling you for a small amount than a large amount; you might not think twice about sending a "friend" $5, but paying $1,500 for a stranger to use your bank account sounds very suspicious. The smaller scams work by targeting thousands of people and hoping that a few of them will fall for it. Don't be one of those people that do.

What to Do if You Get Tricked

I consider myself to be pretty switched on when it comes to scams, but even I've been caught out on the odd occasion. One time, I was on a fake shopping website that tried to capture my card details and another time I had a visit from a fake door-to-door salesman. I didn't lose any money either time, but that was down to sheer dumb luck and it could have ended badly. If you do get scammed, try not to beat yourself up over it. If you act quickly, you might be able to save your money.

If you've been tricked into sending money to a scammer, call your bank right away, tell them it's an unauthorized withdrawal and ask them to reverse it. You can do the same thing if you notice a debit or credit card purchase that you didn't make. This is basically you telling the bank or credit company that it wasn't you who spent that money.

If you check your account and see a purchase that you definitely didn't make, it means that someone else has your debit card information and they can use this to buy things online. You need to cancel your card immediately and the bank will send you a new one with a new number—a bit like changing your password. You can do this through your online banking app, on their website, over the phone, or in the branch.

If you think someone has access to your email, social media accounts, PayPal wallet, or anywhere else where you have personal information, change your password immediately. Pick a new one that has random numbers and letters that aren't easy to guess. You can use an app on your phone to store your passwords if you have trouble remembering them. Here's my favorite trick for creating new passwords that look random but are easy to remember: Find a phrase that you won't forget, like a movie quote or song lyric and take the first letter from each word. For example, "Hello, is it me you're looking for?" becomes Hiimylf. Then add a number and the first two or three letters from the name of the website you're using the password for. So, your password for Amazon would be Hiimylf10ama and your password for PayPal would be Hiimylf10pay. It looks random, but it's actually super simple to remember. Why not give it a go next time you need a new password?

Did you enjoy the book?

Please take a moment to leave a review, as it can greatly benefit the book's visibility. Your review not only supports me, the author (for which I am eternally grateful), but also helps guide other readers searching for a similar book to discover it and has the potential to help someone benefit from the advice offered in this book.

Thank you, your support is greatly appreciated

Kev

A Final Word

GETTING YOUR FIRST JOB is exciting because it brings you new levels of independence and responsibility—two things that teenagers crave because it helps them show the adults in their life how well they're growing up. There's nothing quite like that feeling when you get your first paycheck and you realize that this money is all yours. Maybe you have something in mind that you want to do with it, like taking yourself out for a milkshake and a slice of cake, going on a shopping spree, or putting it toward a larger goal. I can still remember the excitement I felt when I spent the wages from my first full-time paycheck on a stereo system for my bedroom because I knew it would be all mine.

If you've followed the activities and advice in this book, you should be feeling confident about your chances of finally finding work. Whether you fancy marketing your own business or applying to work for someone else with your polished resume, rehearsed interview answers, and superior knowledge of workplace etiquette and acceptable behavior, you should stand out as an excellent candidate, and once you do land that wonderful first job, you'll know how to manage your finances in a mature and responsible fashion.

Of course, even with all your carefully highlighted soft skills, it might take some time before you find the *right* job. Even if you start a job and realize it isn't for you, there'll be a better fit out there somewhere. Don't be disheartened; much like going on a bad date or watching a bad movie, these experiences can still help you learn something. If nothing else, it will give you something to talk about in an interview to show how you've improved and grown from previous mistakes.

Remember to stay positive and keep trying. There's a perfect job out there for everyone, even if you have to invent it yourself!

References

Acas. (2021, March 15). *Sexual harassment*. acas.org.uk. https://www.acas.org.uk/sexual-harassment

Alan Boswell Group. (2022, October 6). *Financial tips for young adults: some of the key tricks to help secure a stable future*. https://www.alanboswell.com/news/financial-tips-for-young-adults-some-of-the-key-tricks-to-help-secure-a-stable-future/

Allingham, T. (2023, May 11). *How much does university cost?*. Save the Student. https://www.savethestudent.org/student-finance/university-study-cost.html)

Apprenticeships. (n.d.). https://www.princes-trust.org.uk/how-we-can-help/tools-resources/finding-job/apprenticeships

Babari, A. (2023, March 3). How can one create a smart career progression strategy. Emeritus. https://emeritus.org/blog/career-career-progression/

TEENS' GUIDE TO FINANCIAL INDEPENDENCE

Be aware of these common financial scams. (2023, October 2). https://www.solveyourdebts.com/blog/financial-scams-to-watch-out-for/

Birt, J. (2023, July 1). *How to write a personal statement on a CV*. Indeed. https://www.indeed.com/career-advice/resumes-cover-letters/how-to-write-a-personal-statement-on-cv

Bringle, L. (2021, August 10). *The 3 main types of credit explained*. Self. https://www.self.inc/blog/types-of-credit

British Youth Council. (2019 June 2). *Youth volunteering*. https://www.byc.org.uk/uk/nhs-youth-forum/youth-volunteering

Caldwell, M. (2022, April 9). *7 signs you don't make enough money*. The Balance. https://www.thebalancemoney.com/signs-you-dont-make-enough-money-2385518

Cherry, K. (2023, November 27). *How to mentally prepare for a full-time job*. Verywell Mind. https://www.verywellmind.com/how-to-mentally-prepare-for-a-full-time-job-5272560

Citizens Advice. (n.d.). *Check your rights at work if you're under 18*. Www.citizensadvice.org.uk. https://www.citizensadvice.org.uk/work/children/check-your-rights-at-work-if-youre-under-18/

Contract of employment guide. (n.d.). https://www.breathehr.com/en-gb/resources/contract-of-employment-guide

Dodson, A. (2023, April 5). *How to find internships in high school (advice from a college intern).* XQ. https://xqsuperschool.org/teaching-learning/how-to-find-an-internship-high-school-college/

8 tips for teaching teens how to save money. (n.d.). https://natwest.mymoneysense.com/parents/articles/8-tips-for-teaching-teens-how-to-save-money/

Federal Trade Commission. (2022, July 16). *What to do if you were scammed.* https://consumer.ftc.gov/articles/what-do-if-you-were-scammed

Frost, A. (2021, August 27). *9 job interview tips for teens to help you land your first (or next) job.* The Muse. https://www.themuse.com/advice/job-interview-tips-for-teens

Future Education Magazine. (2023, August 4). *15 inspirational university quotes to make your college life interesting.* https://futureeducationmagazine.com/inspirational-university-quotes/

GOV.UK. (2012, October 16). *Workplace bullying and harassment.* https://www.gov.uk/workplace-bullying-and-harassment

Green, N. (2024, February 15). *Employed or self-employed – which is better?* Unbiased. https://www.unbiased.co.uk/news/accountant/employed-or-self-employed

Hanson, M. (2023a, October 12). *Average cost of community college*. Education Data Initiative. https://educationdata.org/average-cost-of-community-college

Hanson, M. (2023b, November 18). *Average cost of college* and *tuition*. Education Data Initiative. https://educationdata.org/average-cost-of-college

Healthy work-life balance for teens. (2019, June 7). https://www.educatingmatters.co.uk/blog/healthy-work-life-balance-for-teens/

Hering, B. (2020, December 28). *18 great quotes about work-life balance*. FlexJobs. https://www.flexjobs.com/blog/post/quotes-about-work-life-balance/

How to choose a bank account. (n.d.). https://www.moneyhelper.org.uk/en/everyday-money/banking/how-to-choose-the-right-bank-account

Hunt, M. (2020, January 4). *Young people are getting their first jobs later in life – and it costs them later on.* The Telegraph. https://www.telegraph.co.uk/money/consumer-affairs/young-people-getting-first-jobs-later-life-costs-later/

Indeed Editorial Team. (2021a, November 4). *How to find a job as a teenager (plus benefits and job types)*. https://www.indeed.com/career-advice/finding-a-job/how-to-find-job-as-teenager

Indeed Editorial Team. (2021b December 2). 40 quotes about loving your job that can inspire you. . . https://uk.indeed.com/career-advice/career-development/quotes-about-loving-your.lopment/quotes-about-loving-your-job

Josephson, A. (2023, December 28). *What are income taxes?* Smart Asset. https://smartasset.com/taxes/what-are-income-taxes

Ken Paxton Attorney General of Texas (n.d.). *Common scams*. https://www.texasattorneygeneral.gov/consumer-protection/common-scams

Kerr, E. & Wood, S. (2022, November 3). U*nderstanding financial aid for college: a guide*. US News & World Report. https://www.usnews.com/education/best-colleges/paying-for-college/articles/an-ultimate-guide-to-understanding-college-financial-aid

Lake, R. & Foreman, D. (2021, April 9). T*ypes of bank accounts.* Forbes Advisor. https://www.forbes.com/advisor/banking/what-are-the-different-types-of-bank-accounts/

Modu, E. (2024, January 2). *7 steps to investing as a teenager*. TeenVestor. https://www.teenvestor.com/7steps

Murray, J. (2023, June 20). *What to expect in your first graduate job*. Save the Student. https://www.savethestudent.org/student-jobs/how-to-act-in-your-first-graduate-job.html

Peacock, C. (2022, December 4). *40 quotes to help your child learn the value of money*. GoHenry. https://www.gohenry.com/uk/blog/financial-education/40-quotes-to-help-your-child-learn-the-value-of-money

Perry, E. (2022, October 18). *Full-Time vs. part-time: Which has better benefits?* Betterup. https://www.betterup.com/blog/full-time-vs-part-time-benefits/

Pratt, K. M.. (2023, January 23). *Soft skills*. TechTarget. https://www.techtarget.com/searchcio/definition/soft-skills

Rawhide Youth Services. (2016, June 23). *9 teen job etiquette tips*. https://www.rawhide.org/blog/teen-issues/teen-job-etiquette/

Roney, C. (2022, April 7). *How to find school life balance*. TeenLife. https://www.teenlife.com/blog/how-to-find-school-life-balance/

Share, J. (2017, December 15). *Interview preparation for teens: 11 tips for getting the job*. LiveCareer. https://www.livecareer.com/resources/interviews/prep/teen-job-strategies

Simmons, J. (2021, September 8). *25 jobs for teens and high school students*. Monster . https://www.monster.com/career-advice/article/teen-jobs-0617

Teen workers. (2010, February 22). https://youngworkers.org/rights/teenworkers/

What to do if you've been scammed. (n.d.). https://www.citizensadvice.org.uk/consumer/scams/what-to-do-if-youve-been-scammed/

Willard, M. (2023, March 23). *Teen Time management struggles*. Cadey. https://cadey.co/articles/time-management-in-teens

Youth Employment UK. (2023, April 21). *How to write your first CV*. - step by step guide for students. https://www.youthemployment.org.uk/write-first-cv-tips-students-school-leavers/

About the Author

Having a stark choice of fighting teens on the city streets or helping them find their way in life, Kev Chilton knew which way he wanted to go!

For most of his working life, he was an inner-city cop and detective, concentrating on murder, gun crime, and other serious offences.

However, he joined the police as a 16-year-old cadet and early in his career, he was tasked with helping young offenders, which quickly became his speciality. He noticed that by simply listening to the problems young people were concerned with, the majority were prepared to listen to him back. He built trusting relationships with most, who were happy to listen to and act on his advice. Many responded positively, and they moved confidently into adulthood.

Throughout his police service, he arranged youth clubs, attended schools where he gave talks and maintained an open-door policy, encouraging any young person with a problem to approach him privately afterwards. He also set up and operated specialist juvenile squads geared towards helping those who had gone off the rails. The results were excellent, and he was never happier in his job than when he could redirect a young person's life onto the right path.

It was a fulfilling time in his life, and it helped him understand the constantly evolving challenges teenagers face as they transition to adulthood. More specifically, as times change, so do the needs and circumstances of young people. Choosing the path of mentorship over the chaos of city streets, he has dedicated his journey to helping teenagers, steering them away from conflict and towards a brighter future.

Today, he is proud to utilise his extensive experience to make a positive impact. He is particularly attuned to the unique issues that young people are currently grappling with, and one of his main goals is to bridge the gap between them and the adults in their lives.

Through this series of his guidebooks for teens, Chilton has become an international, award-winning author, and a beacon of support for teenagers and the adults regularly involved with teens.

Today he lives in a converted barn in the beautiful East Kent countryside where family, walking and writing are a big part of his life, and can be reached at :

TEENS' GUIDE TO FINANCIAL INDEPENDENCE

https://kevchilton.com

STAY IN TOUCH

Join our Newsletter <u>School 'n Cool</u> and become part of an amazing community, offering valuable content for Teens, Parents, Teachers

https://kevchilton.com/contact

https://kevchilton.com/contact

Teens' Guide Series

EVERYTHING A TEENAGER NEEDS to tackle the significant challenges and opportunities of adolescence can be found within this series. From friendships and mental health issues to finding employment, managing finances, and developing adult skills, these five books offer practical guidance for teenagers to navigate these crucial years with resilience and strength.

The Teens' Guide Series of books has everything you'll ever need to navigate your teens.

TEENS' GUIDE TO FINANCIAL INDEPENDENCE

Teens' Guide Book Series

Book One  Teens' Guide to Making Friends	Do you find it hard to start conversations or watch others make friends effortlessly? Maybe you just feel awkward and unmotivated. Don't worry—those days are over! Teen's Guide to Making Friends offers strategies to help you talk confidently, navigate social situations, and handle mistakes without stress. This book will boost your social confidence, giving you the tools to create engaging conversations and build new friendships inside, you'll discover how to: ·Overcome insecurities and become a more confident you ·Understand why adults don't always get your struggles ·Become your best self, moving forward Grab your copy of Teen's Guide to Making Friends

KEV CHILTON

Book Two

Teens' Guide to Dating

Are you a teen looking to build healthy relationships, set boundaries, and stay safe while dating online or offline? *Teen's Guide to Dating* is here to help you.

Dating can feel overwhelming, whether you're navigating crushes, breakups, or looking after your own safety. Learn how to find the right partner, create meaningful connections, and stay safe. Inside, you'll discover:

- How to know you're ready to date and build confidence
- Ways to set boundaries, get consent, and confidently communicate your needs
- Tips for LGBT+ dating and different stages of relationships
- Safe sex practices, conflict resolution, and handling breakups

Teen's Guide to Dating gives you the tools to not only enjoy your relationship but also become the best version of yourself. Ready to start your journey? Read now!

Book Three

Teens' Guide to Health & Mental Wellness

Do you ever feel overwhelmed, wondering why life affects you more than your friends? Your feelings are valid, and *Teen's Guide to Self-Care and Wellness* will help you understand and manage them.

Life's stresses can take a toll, but with the right tools, you can navigate them effectively. In this guide, you'll learn to:

- Identify negative mental health indicators
- Master the key ingredients for mental wellness
- Use physical strategies to improve mental health
- Provide first aid for anxiety and depression
- Build your own personal wellness toolbox

Learning to manage stress now will make life easier as you grow. Start your journey to wellness with this guide today!

Book Four

Teens' Guide to Financial Independence

Are you a teen seeking financial independence or a parent wanting to guide your teen? *Teen's Guide to Financial Independence* is your go-to resource for building a successful career and managing your money with confidence.

This comprehensive guide will teach you essential skills for employment and wealth-building. Whether you're just starting or need guidance, this book will be your companion throughout. Inside you'll learn how to:

- Prepare for the world of work and apply for various jobs
- Create a compelling resume and excel in interviews
- Master budgeting, avoid scams, and handle credit cards wisely
- Balance work and life, and plan for university expenses
- Understand investing, saving, and hidden fees

Start to manage *your* finances and secure *your* future, now!

TEENS' GUIDE TO FINANCIAL INDEPENDENCE

Book Five

Teens' Guide to Adult Skills

Ever wondered what secret adults don't tell you about the real world? Find out what that secret is in *Teen's Guide to Adult Skills!* Step into adulthood with confidence and learn how to navigate life's challenges! Inside, you'll discover:

- Activities to improve social skills and resolve conflicts
- Strategies to boost self-confidence, develop a growth mindset, and handle pressure
- Tips for building emotional and social awareness, and connecting after school
- Ready-to-use methods for discovering your passions and creating your own personal development plan
- Tools for setting SMART goals, time management, and handling feedback

Discover your potential and successfully embrace your journey to independence

Get Teen's Guide to Adult Skills today!

https://kevchilton.com/books

www.ingramcontent.com/pod-product-compliance
Lightning Source LLC
Chambersburg PA
CBHW052142070526
44585CB00017B/1935